GEORGE WASHINGTON CARVER

GEORGE WASHINGTON CARVER

A Biography

Gary R. Kremer

GREENWOOD BIOGRAPHIES

 GREENWOOD

AN IMPRINT OF ABC-CLIO, LLC
Santa Barbara, California • Denver, Colorado • Oxford, England

Library of Congress Cataloging-in-Publication Data

Kremer, Gary R.
  George Washington Carver : a biography / Gary R. Kremer.
    p. cm. — (Greenwood biographies)
  Includes bibliographical references and index.
    ISBN 978-0-313-34796-2 (acid-free paper) — ISBN 978-0-313-34797-9
(ebook) 1. Carver, George Washington, 1864?-1943. 2. Agriculturists—
United States—Biography. 3. African American agriculturists—
Biography. 4. Agriculture—Southern States—History—20th century.
5. African American scientists—Biography. I. Title.
  S417.C3K736 2011
  630.92—dc22
  [B]   2010045007

ISBN: 978-0-313-34796-2
EISBN: 978-0-313-34797-9

15 14 13 12 11   1 2 3 4 5

This book is also available on the World Wide Web as an eBook.
Visit www.abc-clio.com for details.

Greenwood
An Imprint of ABC-CLIO, LLC

ABC-CLIO, LLC
130 Cremona Drive, P.O. Box 1911
Santa Barbara, California 93116-1911

This book is printed on acid-free paper ∞

Manufactured in the United States of America

CONTENTS

CONTENTS

SERIES FOREWORD

In response to high school and public library needs, Greenwood developed this distinguished series of full-length biographies specifically for student use. Prepared by field experts and professionals, these engaging biographies are tailored for high school students who need challenging yet accessible biographies. Ideal for secondary school assignments, the length, format, and subject areas are designed to meet educators' requirements and students' interests.

Greenwood offers an extensive selection of biographies spanning all curriculum related subject areas including social studies, the sciences, literature and the arts, history and politics, as well as popular culture, covering public figures and famous personalities from all time periods and backgrounds, both historic and contemporary, who have made an impact on American and/or world culture. Greenwood biographies were chosen based on comprehensive feedback from librarians and educators. Consideration was given to both curriculum relevance and inherent interest. The result is an intriguing mix of the well known and the unexpected, the saints and sinners from long-ago history and contemporary pop culture. Readers will find a wide array of subject choices from fascinating crime figures like Al Capone to inspiring pioneers like Margaret Mead, from the greatest minds of our time like Stephen Hawking to the most amazing success stories of our day like J. K. Rowling.

While the emphasis is on fact, not glorification, the books are meant to be fun to read. Each volume provides in-depth information about the subject's life from birth through childhood, the teen years, and adulthood. A thorough account relates family background and education, traces personal and professional influences, and explores struggles, accomplishments, and contributions. A timeline highlights the most significant life events against a historical perspective. Bibliographies supplement the reference value of each volume.

ACKNOWLEDGMENTS

I have incurred many debts during the nearly three decades that have passed since I began thinking seriously about George Washington Carver and his place in history. I acknowledged the good help I received in producing *George Washington Carver: In His Own Words* in 1987. Another round of "thank yous" is now in order for the help I received in completing this volume.

As is the case with all books, this one builds upon the scholarship of others. My own thinking about George Washington Carver has been informed especially by Linda McMurry's fine biography, *George Washington Carver: Scientist and Symbol* (New York: Oxford University Press, 1981). In my judgment, this book remains the best scholarly work completed to date on Carver. I have also benefited immensely from conversations and correspondence with Linda McMurry Edwards; she is a generous person, as well as a fine scholar. Likewise, Peter Burchard's extensive and very fine work on Carver has been of great help to me. More recently, Mark Hersey has produced a stellar dissertation on Carver as a conservationist. His work is scheduled to be published by the University of Georgia Press early in 2011. As has been the case with Linda McMurry Edwards, Peter Burchard and Mark Hersey have been generous in their willingness to share information and thoughts about the man who all four of us find endlessly intriguing.

Once again, the staff of the George Washington Carver National Monument in Diamond, Missouri, has been unfailingly helpful. In particular, I would like to thank park rangers Lana Henry and Curtis Gregory. Curtis always seemed to be able to find exactly what I was looking for and to do it with great efficiency and good cheer. I also appreciate the Monument's permission to reproduce a modified version of the "Timeline" that its staff has developed as part of its effort to interpret Carver's life. Likewise, Paxton Williams of the George Washington Carver Birthplace Association has been gracious in his willingness to share his vast knowledge of George Washington Carver.

Shirley Baxter, a former student of mine at Lincoln University of Missouri who now works for the National Park Service at the Tuskegee Institute National Historic Site, located in the George Washington Carver Museum on the Tuskegee campus, has also assisted me greatly, especially in identifying and accessing photographs with which to illustrate this book. I am also indebted to the Tuskegee Institute reference archivist, Dana R. Chandler, and his assistant, Roderick Wheeler, for providing images and permission to use them.

Melissa Gottwald and Becky S. Jordan in the Special Collections Department at the Parks Library of Iowa State University Archives, provided me with important information about Carver's career at what was then Iowa State College. I greatly appreciate their prompt and professional assistance.

Librarians and archivists at the Inman E. Page Library on the campus of Lincoln University in Jefferson City, Missouri, have also made my task much easier. Page Library holds a microfilm collection of the papers of George Washington Carver, made available many years ago through a National Historical Publications and Records Commission (NHPRC) grant. I have spent countless hours pouring over the 67 rolls of microfilm that constitute this collection. Head Librarian Liz Wilson, archivist Carmen Beck, and her successor, Mark Schleer, and their assistant, Ithaca Bryant, have done all that they could to make my task easier. I have also been assisted greatly by the holdings and the staff of the Elmer Ellis Library on the University of Missouri campus.

My editor at Greenwood Press/ABC-CLIO, Sandy Towers, has been incredibly patient with my failure to meet multiple deadlines. Always she has been supportive and encouraging, for which I thank her immensely.

Likewise, my coworkers at The State Historical Society of Missouri and the Western Historical Manuscript Collection have tolerated my obsession with George Washington Carver over the past few years. I have appreciated their willingness to listen to my ramblings even when I know they had better things to do. The executive committee of the Society's Board of Trustees encouraged me to complete this book. I could not have done so without the latitude they provided me within my job. I am deeply indebted to all members of the committee, especially past president Doug Crews and current president Stephen N. Limbaugh Jr.

Finally, I want to thank my family for putting up with the Carver clutter in my house and in my mind while this book has been under construction. That includes not only my wife, Lisa, but also our children and their spouses: Randy (Michaela), Sharon Bax (Travis), and Becky Dazey (Jeff). I have tried not to allow my work on this book to interfere with my time with grandchildren Dustin, Brooke, and Bladen Kremer and Logan, Kaden, Halston, and Saylor Bax. If I have failed in that effort, I apologize to them. I have written this book as much for them as for anyone.

I apologize in advance for any errors in fact or judgment that may have found their way into this book in spite of all the good help I have received. The fault for any such shortcomings remains my own.

TIMELINE: EVENTS IN THE LIFE OF GEORGE WASHINGTON CARVER

1891–1896 Attends Iowa State College in Ames, Iowa.

1896 Begins work at Tuskegee Institute as Director of Agricultural Experiment Station; U.S. Supreme Court issues *Plessy v. Ferguson* decision, upholding segregation.

1906 Initiates Jesup Wagon.

1915 Booker T. Washington dies; replaced as principal by Robert Russa Moton.

1916 Elected Fellow of the Royal Society for the Encouragement of Arts, London, England.

1917 United States enters World War I.

1921 Appears before U.S. House of Representatives, Committee on Ways and Means, for tariff on peanuts.

1923 Recipient, Spingarn Medal for Distinguished Service in Agricultural Science.

1928 Receives honorary degree, Doctor of Science, Simpson College.

1929 Stock market crash; beginning of Great Depression.

1935 Appointed Collaborator with USDA with Mycology and Plant Disease Survey.

1937 Bronze bust of Carver unveiled at Tuskegee Institute.

1939 Receives Roosevelt Medal for Outstanding Contribution to Southern Agriculture.

1941 George Washington Carver Museum dedicated at Tuskegee Institute; United States enters World War II.

1943 Carver dies at Tuskegee Institute, Alabama; Congress authorizes George Washington Carver National Monument.

1947 Carver postage stamp issued.

1951 George Washington Carver National Monument established, Diamond, Missouri.

1953 Dedication of Carver National Monument.

1954 U.S. Supreme Court's *Brown v. Board of Education* decision outlaws segregation in schools.

1956 Simpson College dedicates science building in Carver's honor.

1966 Polaris submarine *George Washington Carver* launched.

1968 Iowa State College dedicated science building in memory of George Washington Carver.

1969 Elected to Agricultural Hall of Fame, Kansas City, Kansas.

1973 Elected to Hall of Fame for Great Americans.

1995 Awarded the Missourian Award.

1996 Receives honorary degree from Highland College, Kansas.

1999 USDA dedicates George Washington Carver Center, Beltsville, Maryland.

2002 Receives the Iowa Award.

2006 Missouri names state agriculture building for Carver.

Chapter 1

EARLY YEARS

An orphan child of a race that is considered inferior from every angle.

—*George Washington Carver, letter to Mr. Gordon Besch*

Any account of the life and accomplishments of the distinguished African American scientist George Washington Carver must begin with a description and explanation of the challenging circumstances surrounding his birth and early life. It would be difficult to imagine how he could have been born at a more dangerous time, in a more threatening place, under more challenging circumstances.

The exact date of Carver's birth has been disputed for more than a century. Even he remained unsure of his birth date. In a memoir written in "1897 or thereabouts," he reported, "As nearly as I can trace my history I was about 2 weeks old when the [Civil] war closed."[1] That would place his birth date in the early spring of 1865, perhaps in late March or early April. In a second reminiscence, written some 25 years later, Carver reported that "I was born in Diamond Grove, Mo., about the close of the great Civil War."[2]

Still later in his life, Carver often reported his birth year as 1864, although he offered no evidence to support that date. His uncertainty about exactly when he was born, his inability to establish a definitive date, and the fact that his birth was such an inauspicious event that no one recorded or remembered its occurrence were factors that could have scarred and stifled him for life. He was, after all, one of more than 100,000 African Americans living in Missouri, a state where for decades blacks were regarded as property before the law and as inferior to even the lowest class of whites.

Carver's mother was a slave named Mary, owned by an Ohio-born couple, Moses and Susan Carver, who moved to Newton County, in the far southwest corner of Missouri, during the late 1830s, making them among the earliest white settlers in the area. The Carvers acquired Mary in 1855, their alleged hostility toward the institution of slavery overridden by their need for help in a land where free persons' labor was scarce and expensive. The 1860 federal slave schedule for Newton County suggests that Mary was 20 years old in that year and that she was the mother of an infant son, George's older brother, James. She was one of 426 slaves in a county whose population numbered more than nine thousand people.[3]

Carver's father, he later learned, "was the property of Mr. Grant, who owned the adjoining plantation," by which, no doubt, he meant "farm."[4] There were no Old South-like plantations in Newton County. Missouri's "Black Belt," the area of the state where the largest number of slaves lived, lay roughly 200 miles north, in the fertile Missouri River valley known as the "Boonslick." The "Mr. Grant" to whom Carver referred was likely James Grant, a North Carolina native who was 75 years old in 1860 and the owner of two male slaves, one 46 years old in 1860, the other Mary's age in the same year. While either of those men, or even Moses Carver, could have been George's father, it seems likely that the younger man would have served that role. George's father, whose name he apparently never knew, was killed in an accident before the future scientist was even born. Carver's dark skin color and heavily "black" features, in contrast to the lightly colored Jim, suggests, but does not prove, that the two boys had different fathers.

Moses and Susan Carver, the white couple who owned the black Carvers, were 47 and 46 years old, respectively, in 1860. Living in their household in that year, in addition to Mary and James, was a

22-year-old Missouri-born white man named Jackson Carroll, who worked on the farm as a laborer. As such, he was the principal assistant to Moses Carver on the southwest Missouri prairie land farm that consisted of 220 acres of unimproved land and 100 acres of improved land. The 1860 agricultural census suggests that the Carver family subsisted on the farm's produce, with relatively little being raised for a market economy. In 1860, the Carvers owned 11 horses, at least some of which, according to local lore, were "race horses"; 4 "milch" cows that produced 200 pounds of butter; and 11 head of "other" cattle. The farm's major crop was Indian corn; Carver raised 1,000 bushels of it, most if not all of which would have been consumed by his livestock. He also raised 200 bushels of oats. Eleven sheep produced 24 pounds of wool, and bees owned by the Carvers produced 200 pounds of honey. Moses Carver slaughtered his own meat, including 1 or more of his 15 head of swine. The farm was, indeed, a relatively small operation, but, as historian Mark Hersey points out, "In light of Carver's later work, it is worth at least noting that Moses had also provided an object lesson to George in the benefits of diversified farming."[5]

The Civil War, which officially began with the Confederate firing on Fort Sumter in South Carolina, on April 12, 1861, was an especially fratricidal conflict in deeply divided Missouri. The state's governor, Governor Claiborne Fox Jackson, one of Saline County, Missouri's largest slave owners, sought to move the state into the Confederacy in the wake of President Abraham Lincoln's election in the fall of 1860. Lincoln, the candidate who opposed the expansion of slavery, garnered only 22 votes in Newton County out of nearly 1,400 votes cast. Interestingly, the secessionist candidate, John C. Breckenridge of Kentucky, received more than 10 times the number of votes that Lincoln earned. Union Democrat Stephen A. Douglas of Illinois carried both the state and the county, although in Newton County more voters cast votes for his three opponents than for him.

When a state convention held in St. Louis in March 1861 refused to allow the state to secede from the Union, Governor Jackson tried to effect the state's secession on his own. In his inaugural address earlier that year, Jackson had called for Missourians to stand by their sister states of the Confederacy and raise an army to resist Union aggression.

Eventually, that sort of rhetoric and action became more than the pro-Union forces in Missouri could tolerate, and Governor Jackson was driven from the capital city by Union soldiers under the command of General Nathaniel Lyon in June 1861. Governor Jackson tried some months later to set up a rump government in the Newton County seat of Neosho, where Confederate general Sterling Price occupied the town for a time, before moving on to Arkansas and later Texas. Jackson died in exile in 1862, still convinced he was Missouri's legitimate governor.

Many Missourians, although certainly not a majority, continued to support Jackson and the Confederate cause throughout the war years, even though Missouri remained officially in the Union. Bloodshed, violence, and mayhem reigned in Missouri throughout the four-year conflict and beyond. Cousins, brothers, fathers, and sons often found themselves on opposite sides of the fight, especially along Missouri's western border, which separated it from Free Soil Kansas.

Much violence and destruction occurred in Newton County, where Carver was born, during the Civil War, as well. After all, nearly 3,000 of Newton County's 8,895 residents in 1860 were born in the southern states of Tennessee, Kentucky, North Carolina, or Virginia. The county was the location of a hard-fought contest between Union and Confederate sympathizers in September 1862. Known as the Battle of Newtonia, this fight was a decisive Confederate victory, a battle in which at least 50 Union soldiers were killed and 80 or more captured. But that battle was only the most pronounced and visible of the conflicts that occurred in the county during the war. Guerrilla violence by supporters of both sides was common during the war, and some southwest Missourians used the war to settle old scores, real or imagined. People were robbed and killed and property stolen. Private and public buildings, including the county courthouse, were destroyed. The market economy was left in shambles.[6]

Missouri's Union provost marshal, the military authority in the Show-Me State, reviewed 178 cases in Newton County alone during the war, an average of nearly 1 per week during the four years of fighting. Many of these cases had to do with questions about citizens' loyalty to the Union. Others dealt with charges of violence against Newton County residents and/or the destruction or theft of property. Early in the war, a series of cases documented a fight over control of a lead smelting operation at nearby Granby, and, in late 1863, the provost marshal addressed the charge that a marauding band of uncertain allegiance had robbed a smallpox hospital near Newtonia, taking food and clothing and small arms from a nearby house.[7]

The Battle of Newtonia occurred less than 30 miles from the Moses Carver farm in Newton County. The war came directly to the Carver household on multiple occasions, first in 1862, when Moses Carver was purportedly accosted by marauders who strung him up by his thumbs from a walnut tree in an attempt to force him to tell where he had allegedly buried a cache of gold. Whether this attack really occurred and whether or not Carver possessed any gold, this incident remained an important part of Carver family lore long after its alleged or real occurrence.

Still later in the war, not long after George's birth, another band of armed men attacked the Carver household. This time, instead of trying to steal money, they stole two of Carver's slaves, the young woman named Mary and her infant child, George. Moses Carver apparently had time to hide George's older brother, James. According to an account of the event written by Carver in 1922, he reported that the thieves "carried my mother and myself down into Arkansas, and sold my mother." Moses Carver hired someone to try to retrieve mother and son, but the man was able only to return the infant George to his master. Carver's account of the story, presumably as told to him by his former master, was that his return to the Moses Carver farm cost Mr. Carver a prized race horse worth $300.[8] The retelling of this story, confirming as it did the lack of regard for the humanity of an infant slave, could simply have nurtured Carver's harsh understanding that he had once been regarded as property, rather than as a person. Instead, however, Carver seems to have taken pride in the notion that his master bothered to retrieve him and that Moses Carver was willing to do so at the cost of a valuable horse at a time when the state of Missouri had either already abolished slavery or was getting ready to do so.

Young George tried for years to find his mother and suffered her loss throughout his life. Late into his life, he regarded as his most prized possessions the bill of sale that made his mother the property of the Carvers and a spinning wheel that had belonged to her.

Not only did George no longer have his mother to care for him, but he was returned to the Carver household near death, suffering from whooping cough. Although he survived that bout of illness, he remained sickly throughout his childhood. One of his contemporaries, Forbes Brown, recalled in late life that Carver was so frail as a child that he always assumed that George simply did not get enough to eat. George remembered that he was small for his age as a child and that "my body was very feble [sic] and it was a constant warfare between life and death to see who would gain the mastery." This reality notwithstanding, Carver eventually grew to a height of six feet.[9]

What must George's life have been like, growing up in the household of a late-middle-aged white couple in a township that contained only 16 African Americans in 1870 among a total population of 1,166 residents? Carver rarely spoke or wrote in detail about his childhood. Late in life, when pressed to do so by biographer Rackham Holt, he responded simply that "It will be very difficult indeed" to recall his early life in detail, "as there are so many things that naturally I erased from my mind." He added, "There are some things that an orphan child does not want to remember."[10] On at least two other occasions late in his life, Carver made similar comments to would-be biographers, suggesting the weight of the burden he felt of being "an orphan child of a race that is considered inferior from every angle."[11] Similarly, Carver told another writer who sought to learn more details of his childhood, "It may seem odd to you that these things are so vague in my mind. Naturally to the average white child they would be events in his life, but to a frail orphan colored child who had to meet disappointment often many times per day no attempt was made to remember such incidents." "In fact," he added, "a number of things we try to forget."[12]

This reluctance or inability to remember, however, should not be taken to mean that George and his brother, Jim, were mistreated by the Carvers or that the boys bore hostility toward them. There are a number of indications that the white Carvers regarded their former slaves as surrogate children and that they treated them with kindness and even affection. A professional portrait of George as a young boy and another of George and Jim together in their youth, no doubt paid for by Moses and Susan, suggest parental pride that transcended any purely economic relationship. Like many other former slaves in Missouri, Jim stayed with the Carver family for more than a decade after slavery ended and retained the Carver surname into adulthood. Moreover, George returned to Newton County on multiple occasions to visit his former masters. At least one biographer reported that, later in life, after he had gone to work at Tuskegee Institute, Carver sometimes purchased overalls and work shirts to be sent to Moses Carver and also sent "numerous postal money orders for small amounts, usually five or ten dollars" to his former master.[13]

Further evidence of George Carver's childhood contentment comes in his correspondence during the 1920s with Eva Goodwin, a Newton County native who was the daughter of one of Moses Carver's grand-nephews, a man who had been George's boyhood playmate. In a letter to Mrs. Goodwin, George told her that her recent correspondence "causes tears to come to my eyes as I recall childhood's happy days." He also told Mrs. Goodwin that he loved her father "as I did my own brother." Later, in another letter, he told her, "I would love to get with your Father and talk over old times at home," adding, "you really are my home folks."[14]

Carver's childhood fragility and frequent illnesses limited his ability to work outdoors on the Carver farm; that responsibility was assigned to his older brother, James. The Carver farm seems, in fact, to have declined in productivity and prosperity during the Civil War decade, as was the case in many parts of wartorn Missouri. Federal census returns for 1870 reveal that by that date, the aging Moses Carver had fewer horses, milch cows, and other cattle than he had had 10 years earlier. He did have more sheep (35) than he had in 1860 and the same number of swine (15), although he produced only half the corn and none of the oats he had harvested in 1860.

While James was helping Moses Carver in the fields, George was assigned to help Aunt Susan, who taught him to do household chores, such as cooking, cleaning, sewing, and all of the tasks associated with laundry, including ironing. Those skills would serve him well throughout the remainder of his life.

Perhaps it was George's assisting Aunt Susan with gardening that nurtured his seemingly innate fascination with plants. In an 1897 reminiscence, he reported that flowers especially intrigued him: "Day after day I spent in the woods alone in order to collect my floral beautis [sic]."

Often, he transplanted these flowers into a small, hidden garden that he maintained out of sight of the Carvers, because "it was considered foolishness in that neighborhood to waste time on flowers." Occasionally, George's effort at transplantation failed, leaving him emotionally distraught: "[M]any are the tears I have shed because I would break the roots or flower of some of my pets while removing them from the ground."[15]

Plants thrived under the child Carver's care. At least in his telling of the story, he became known as the community "plant doctor," and neighbors brought sickly plants to him. Carver remembered that "all sorts of vegetation succeed[ed] to thrive under my touch," an experience that must have nurtured his notion that he was a special person with extraordinary powers and abilities. That notion remained with and guided him throughout his life.[16]

Carver did not attend school as a very young child. There was no state compulsory-education law in Missouri when he was of elementary school age. Indeed, Missouri law required blacks and whites to be edu-

George Carver's unusual abilities were recognized in his boyhood, yet as an African American in post–Civil War rural Missouri, he had very limited access to formal schooling. (Courtesy of the Tuskegee University Archives)

cated separately, and townships were not required to provide schools for blacks unless there were at least 15 (later 20) black school-age children in the political subdivision. Fewer than 10 black children of school age, including Carver, lived in Newton County's Marion Township in 1870. There is some evidence that George and Jim tried to attend a local white school near the Carver farm but were prohibited from doing so by both law and custom.[17]

Still, the curious Carver learned to read and write at an early age, helped, apparently, by Aunt Susan, with whom he seemed to have a strong bond. Although some sources have suggested that Moses Carver was illiterate, the 1870 and 1880 federal census returns suggest otherwise. George's only book, he reported in 1922, "was an old Webster's Elementary Spelling Book," which he "almost knew . . . by heart." More often than not, however, the book was unable to answer the many questions that filled the young Carver's mind. Years later, Carver summed up his early intellectual curiosity by commenting simply that "From a child I had an inordinate desire for knowledge."[18]

Carver's thirst for knowledge led him to leave his early childhood home as an adolescent. Thus began more than a decade of wandering by a young man who seemed to be in search not only of formal education but also of a destiny. He remembered years later that the Carvers supported his decision, explaining, "Mr. and Mrs. Carver were perfectly willing for us to go where we could be educated the same as white children."[19]

The Carvers heard that there was a school for blacks in the county seat of Neosho, a town of about 3,000 persons, some eight miles away. George set out on foot to become a student in that school. He was approximately 12 years of age when he did so.

At that point in his life, the boy Carver had rarely been off the Carver farm and certainly had never been out of the county of his birth, save for the kidnapping episode that had occurred during his infancy. It is difficult to imagine the complex of emotions he must have felt as he set out on the three-hour walk to Neosho. He apparently knew no one in the town, had rarely visited there, and surely must have felt anxiety about being on his own with no money, no resources upon which he could draw, and not even a place to stay when he arrived at his destination. Still, he must also have been excited at the thought of the adventure that he was embarking upon and the prospect of at last getting a chance to go to school.

Arriving in Neosho after dark, Carver spotted a barn and decided to sleep in it for the night. The next morning, he realized that his choice of locations had been a good one; the barn was owned by Andrew and Mariah Watkins, a childless black couple who agreed to provide George with room and board in exchange for his help with chores.[20]

The Neosho in which Carver found himself living during the mid- to late 1870s was a thriving, fast-growing community of roughly 3,300 persons, approximately 400 of whom were identified in the 1880 federal census as either "black" or "mulatto." Thus, African Americans constituted roughly 12 percent of Neosho's population, a considerable increase over the previous decade. In 1870, Neosho's total population was 2,023,129 (6%) of whom were African Americans. This was only a slight increase over the 106 slaves in Neosho in 1860.[21]

Why the African American population of Neosho more than tripled during the decade of the 1870s remains a mystery, although it was common during the war years in Missouri for African Americans to flee the rural countryside in search of greater security and job opportunities in towns and villages. Regardless, it must have been quite a sight for the young Carver to see hundreds of people who looked like himself walking the streets of the town.

Mariah Watkins seems to have influenced Carver in a number of ways, even though he lived in the Watkins home only a short period of time. "Aunt" Mariah took in laundry for hire and required George to help her, thereby forcing him to hone a skill that he would employ for his own survival many times over the next decade or more. She also served the community as a midwife and home remedyist. Her knowledge of plants and their purported curative powers appealed to George and, no doubt, laid the groundwork for his lifelong conviction that illnesses could be cured through the proper use of plants and the products that could be extracted from them. No doubt, the lesson of Aunt Mariah's positive relationship with Neosho whites, born of her ability to provide services whites needed, was not lost on young George.[22]

Yet another way in which Aunt Mariah influenced George was through her regular reading of the Bible and her encouraging George to do likewise. Many years later, in the seventh decade of his life,

Carver wrote to a would-be biographer about his religious conversion as a young child: "I was just a mere boy when converted, hardly ten years old. . . . God just came into my heart while I was alone in the 'loft' of our big barn while I was shelling corn to carry to the mill to be ground into meal." Subsequently, Carver remembered, "A dear little white boy, one of our neighbors, about my age came by one Saturday morning and in talking and playing he told me he was going to Sunday school tomorrow morning." Carver wanted to know what a Sunday school was. The boy told him it was a place where people sang hymns and prayed. Unfamiliar with the concept of prayer, Carver waited until the boy left. Then, he recalled, "I knelt down by the barrel of corn and prayed as best I could." Later, he attended a Sunday school class intermittently as a child. Moses and Susan Carver, by contrast, were not churchgoers.[23]

According to one of his contemporaries, George was heavily influenced by a Sunday school teacher, Mrs. Flora Abbott. Widely known for her fondness of children and her knowledge of the Bible, Mrs. Abbott "constantly stressed the fact that the Lord heard and answered the prayers of a child just as surely as He did that of their parents."[24]

Mrs. Abbott encouraged members of her class to pray and to believe that their prayers were answered. George became one of Mrs. Abbott's star pupils, and she rewarded his studiousness and attentiveness with gifts and praise. While still a child, he apparently developed what became a lifelong practice of rising before dawn and walking in the woods to talk with God and to know Him better through His creations.[25]

Carver's conversion to Christianity gave him a sense of a deeply personal relationship with God, who, he was convinced, frequently spoke to him through dreams and other forms of direct revelation. His earliest recollection of such an experience, one that he often spoke about throughout his life, came through a childhood dream. Longing for a pocketknife of his own, George dreamed of a knife sticking in a partially eaten watermelon in one of Moses Carver's fields. Upon waking the next morning, George walked to the spot on the farm revealed to him in his sleep. There, he saw the scene he had just dreamed of—the object of his longing, a knife sticking in a partially eaten watermelon. The experience made a firm believer of him: dreams were to be believed, and God was to be trusted.[26]

In Neosho, in addition to encouraging George's Bible study, Mariah Watkins also took him to regular church services at the local African Methodist Episcopal church. Religion remained a dominant, shaping force in Carver's life for the rest of his years.

Once settled in with the Watkins family in Neosho, Carver enrolled almost at once in the town's "colored school," a one-room schoolhouse adjacent to the Watkins's home and named for the slain 16th president of the United States. Established in 1872, the school was taught by Stephen Frost, a young black man, probably in his mid-twenties, who likely had little or no formal training as a teacher. Sometimes an ability to recite the ABCs was the only qualification that a black teacher in postwar Missouri had to possess. Some critics of the black educational system at the time argued that even that expectation often went unenforced.[27]

The illiteracy rate among African Americans in Missouri remained high during the generation following the Civil War, one legacy of the prewar prohibition against teaching blacks, slave or free, to read or write. Before the war, whites opposed educating blacks, fearing that literacy would lead to unrest, dissatisfaction, and rebellion. After the war, many whites opposed public funding for black schools, angry at the notion that they were required to pay taxes for the education of black freedmen, whom they regarded as their intellectual and social inferiors. In some counties, schoolhouses for African Americans were burned, teachers of black students were verbally and physically abused, and county officials tried to find ways to avoid their legal responsibility for establishing schools for blacks, including refusing to report or underreporting the number of black school-age children in the county.

The lack of educated blacks in postwar Missouri, the reluctance of black parents to have their children taught by white teachers, whom they tended not to trust, and the white hostility toward educating blacks at public expense meant that qualified African American teachers were hard to find and well-equipped schools for blacks were almost nonexistent, especially in rural and small-town Missouri.

Carver did not stay long in Neosho, perhaps less than a year. Stephen Frost and the Lincoln School apparently had little to offer him. Wanderlust struck Carver, prompting him to want to leave Missouri for Kansas, a place regarded by many former slave-state African Americans as "the promised land" because of its historical association with the abolitionist John Brown.

By the late 1870s, thousands of southern blacks began to move up the Mississippi River to various points in Missouri, from which they traveled overland to Kansas in search of a better life. They were fleeing the South in the wake of the so-called Compromise of 1877, a political deal between congressional leaders that allowed Republican Rutherford B. Hayes to become president of the United States in exchange for the removal of the federal troops remaining in the South, sent there after the war to protect the civil and political rights of African Americans. This so-called Exodus, named to commemorate and identify with the flight of Jews from their captivity in Egypt to freedom in Israel, marked the end of Reconstruction in the South and the re-emergence there of state governments that were hostile to African Americans' efforts to enjoy social and political equality.[28]

Carver seems to have hitched a ride sometime in 1878 or 1879 with a black Exoduster family passing through Missouri en route to Kansas. No more than 14 or 15 years old at the time and still with few resources available to him to start a new life, George Carver joined what became the first major migration out of the South by African Americans. Like all of the other migrants, Carver was in search of a better life.

He took with him, of course, the sum of his experiences in Missouri. Although an African American orphan reared in a community and state that regarded blacks as less than equal to whites, he had been aided and cared for by whites who were genuinely fond of him and perhaps even loved him. He had developed a sense that he possessed unique gifts and that he had a specialness that transcended race, a feeling no doubt nurtured by his Christian conversion experience and the treatment he received from his Sunday school teacher. Equally important, he took with him Moses Carver's "abhorrence of waste." Historian Mark Hersey has noted, "Moses possessed an intense distaste for waste of any kind despite the abundance of natural resources at his disposal," a distaste that he no doubt passed on to George and which the latter nurtured throughout his life.[29] Given all of his experiences and the confident hope that must have sprung from them, the teenage Carver must have been excited indeed.

NOTES

1. Quoted in Gary R. Kremer, ed., *George Washington Carver: In His Own Words* (Columbia: University of Missouri Press, 1987), 20.

2. Ibid., 23.

3. Linda O. McMurry, *George Washington Carver: Scientist and Symbol* (New York: Oxford University Press, 1981), 5. The 1860 slave schedule for Newton County, Missouri, may be accessed through Ancestry.com.

4. Kremer, *George Washington Carver*, 23.

5. Mark D. Hersey, "'My Work Is That of Conservation': The Environmental Vision of George Washington Carver," Ph.D. diss., University of Kansas, 2006, 29.

6. Edward C. Bearss, "The Army of the Frontier's First Campaign: The Confederates Win at Newtonia," *Missouri Historical Review* 60 (April 1966): 283–319.

7. The index to the Missouri Unionist Provost Marshal Papers, 1861–1865, may be accessed at http://www.sos.mo.gov/archives/provost.

8. Kremer, *George Washington Carver*, 23.

9. Robert P. Fuller and Merrill J. Mattes, "The Early Life of George Washington Carver," unpublished manuscript, George Washington Carver National Monument, Diamond, Missouri, November 1957, 29; Kremer, *George Washington Carver*, 20.

10. Kremer, *George Washington Carver*, 31.

11. George Washington Carver to Gordon Besch, November 9, 1937, GWC Papers, microfilm edition, compiled and filmed by the National Historical Publication Commission, 1975, Inman E. Page Library, Lincoln University, Jefferson City, MO, Roll 22, frame 0482. Hereafter referred to as "GWC Papers." The original GWC Papers are housed at the Tuskegee Institute Archives in Alabama.

12. George Washington Carver to T. H. Alexander, December 16, 1937, GWC Papers, Roll 22, frame 0670.

13. Ethel Edwards, *Carver of Tuskegee* (Cincinnati, OH: Psyche Press, 1971), 70–71.

14. Quoted in Kremer, *George Washington Carver*, 39–41.

15. Ibid., 20–21.

16. Ibid.

17. McMurry, *George Washington Carver*, 18.

18. Kremer, *George Washington Carver*, 20, 23.

19. Ibid., 23.

20. McMurry, *George Washington Carver*, 20–21.

21. These figures are gleaned from federal census returns that can be accessed through Ancestry.com.

22. McMurry, *George Washington Carver*, 20, 27.

23. George Washington Carver to Isabelle Coleman, July 24, 1931, GWC Papers, Roll 12, frames 1264–1265.

24. Fuller and Mattes, "The Early Life of George Washington Carver," 27–28.

25. Ibid.

26. The most famous retelling of this story appears in Glenn Clark, *The Man Who Talks with the Flowers: The Life Story of Dr. George Washington Carver* (Austin, MN: Macalester Park, 1939), 22.

27. McMurry, *George Washington Carver*, 20–21.

28. The best source on the so-called Exodus remains Nell Irvin Painter, *Exodusters: Black Migration to Kansas after Reconstruction* (New York: Knopf, 1977).

29. Hersey, "'My Work Is That of Conservation,'" 9, 25.

Chapter 2

WANDERING AND WONDERING

I trusted God and pushed ahead.

—*George Washington Carver, "A Brief Sketch of My Life"*

George Carver left Missouri sometime during the late 1870s, headed for Fort Scott, Kansas, walking the 90-plus miles alongside a wagon in the company of other African Americans in search of a better life and greater opportunity in the land of "free Kansas." Likely, he was not yet 15 years old. Like a great many other Exodusters, Carver probably assumed that Kansans were less racially bigoted than were residents of former slave states. Although over the next decade he would have occasion to question that assumption more than once, he would also discover that whites would be among his greatest benefactors.

Carver's first home in Kansas was in the household of Felix Payne, a Tennessee-born African American who worked as a blacksmith in Fort Scott. Payne was in his early thirties in the late 1870s, his wife, Mattie, in her late twenties. Payne's Kentucky-born mother-in-law also shared the household, which seems to have been located in a largely white neighborhood. The addition of a boarder such as Carver in a household that already contained an extended family member was common in African American households during the generation after the Civil War, one of the many ways in which blacks sought to survive the challenges of freedom in an economically competitive society. Reflecting its popularity as an Exoduster destination, Fort Scott saw its black population grow from 682 persons in 1870 to 1,083 in 1880, a growth rate of nearly 60 percent. By contrast, the town's white population grew by less than 30 percent during the same period.[1]

No doubt this significant increase in black population exacerbated racial tension. Early in 1879, tension led to violence in Fort Scott, resulting in the lynching of a black man in an incident witnessed by Carver. Over the course of the next two decades, racial lynching became an increasingly common phenomenon, less so in the Midwest than in the South but still all too common even in the American heartland.

The lynching that Carver witnessed took place on the night of March 26, 1879, in the wake of the alleged rape of a young white girl by a black man. The accused rapist was dragged from the county jail by a group of masked men, rooted on by a crowd of hundreds, perhaps as many as a thousand. The mob secured a rope around its victim's neck, dragged him for blocks, and then hanged him from a lamppost until he was dead. Not yet satisfied, the mob proceeded to burn the man's body in a public act of desecration and lawlessness that left other African Americans, including Carver, horrified and afraid. He left town immediately. Years later, as an old man, he briefly recalled the incident to biographer Rackham Holt, writing simply, "Remained [in Fort Scott] until they linched [sic] a colored man, drug him by our house and dashed his brains out onto the sidewalk. As young as I was, the horror haunted me and does even now. I left Fort Scott and went to Olathe, Kansas."[2]

It is impossible to overemphasize the terror that Carver and other African Americans felt at the sight of this lynching—the wanton and barbaric murder and mutilation of a black man in broad daylight by a group of men who clearly felt no fear of reprisal, legal or otherwise. The incident must have solidified Carver's sense for the need to accommodate whites and to treat them with the utmost deference, even, perhaps especially, when they least deserved it.

From Fort Scott, Carver moved 82 miles due north to Olathe, just west of Kansas City. Apparently he enrolled again in school while living with another African American couple, C. C. and Lucy Seymour, both of whom were Virginia-born and in their late forties. During the mid-1950s, a National Park Service employee interviewed Rashey B. Moten, a Carver contemporary, who attended school in Olathe with young George. Moten remembered that he and George "finished the fourth grade together." Moten described George as "A tall, lanky kid," who "didn't care to play many games." George, Moten recalled, preferred inspecting and collecting plants and leaves of trees to playing marbles.[3]

While living with the Seymours, Carver did odd jobs, including cooking and shoe shining, while also assisting Lucy Seymour, who took in laundry for hire. Carver also began to teach a Sunday school class at the local Methodist church in Olathe, a town of just under 4,000 people, fewer than 250 of whom were African American.[4]

Early in 1880, the Seymours moved to Minneapolis, Kansas. Carver subsequently moved in with yet another black couple, Willis and Delilah Moore, who lived in Paola, about 25 miles from Olathe. The federal census taker caught up with him there during the summer of 1880. According to the census, Carver was a 15-year-old boarder in the Moore household, whose other residents included the couple's daughter, son, mother, and nephew. Willis Moore and the couple's children were described in the census as "Mulatto," while the others in the household, including George, were listed as "black."[5]

The census also reveals that George gave his birthplace as Missouri but that he was unable to provide the birthplaces of his parents. He gave his occupation as "Works in laundry" and indicated he had been enrolled in school during the current year.

From Paola, Carver traveled to Minneapolis, Kansas, following the Seymours, with whom he seems to have developed a close bond. Carver spent the next four years in Minneapolis, a town of slightly more than 1,000 people, fewer than 20 of whom were African American. He lived at least part of the time with the Seymours and operated a laundry business, financed with money borrowed on at least three occasions from a local bank, in an area of the town known as "Poverty Gulch." It is worth noting that Carver, a young black man, who clearly had few if any assets, secured these loans from white bankers when he was not yet 20 years old. Another contemporary, Chester Rarig, recalled a number of years later that Carver lived and worked out of a "shack [that] had been abandoned by some white family. . . . George took possession and revamped it somewhat making it habitable."[6]

Life seems to have been good for Carver in Minneapolis. He attended school there in a two-story, four-room frame building and apparently impressed his white classmates and their teacher with the depth and breadth of his knowledge of a number of subjects. Years later, Nellie Davis Cawley remembered attending school with George, who, she recalled, entered her school as an eighth-grade student. In 1922, Carver recalled Minneapolis, Kansas, as the place "where I finished my high school work."[7]

Although Cawley remembered Carver well, she also recalled that he "was very different from other colored children we knew," adding, "He was quiet and did not mix with others in the playground. He would just stand and look around." Others, however, remembered him as having a playful, open personality that attracted many friends, mostly white, and that he was a frequent dinner guest in white homes. Indeed, he seems almost to have been a novelty in this mostly white town—a talented and educated black man who posed no threat to whites or their system of racial hierarchy.[8]

While in Minneapolis, Carver "was admitted by examination" into the Presbyterian church to which the Seymours belonged. One suspects that his decision to abandon his African Methodist Episcopal roots to become a Presbyterian had little to do with doctrine and everything to do with his friendship with the Seymours. Carver honed a number of his talents while in Minneapolis, including painting, crocheting, and playing the mouth harp and the accordion. He also acquired his middle initial, "W," while there, an addition that he made to ensure that his mail did not go to another George Carver living in the community. Although Carver later came to be known as "George Washington Carver," he apparently did not intend the "W" to stand for anything other than a middle initial.[9]

While in Minneapolis, George learned of the death of his only known living blood relative, his brother, Jim, who had died of smallpox sometime after leaving Moses Carver's farm during the early 1880s to seek greater economic opportunity in Arkansas. Although Jim and George had not seen each other for several years and apparently had not stayed in contact by means of letters, George took Jim's death hard. Years later, in his 1922 memoir, he commented on his brother's death with the stoicism that he had learned to employ in difficult circumstances: "The sad news reached me . . . that James, my only brother had died. . . . Being conscious as never before that I was left alone, I trusted God and pushed ahead."[10]

Despite his relatively pleasant stay in Minneapolis, Carver left the town in 1884, struck again by the wanderlust that seemed still to affect him. After selling two town lots that he had purchased earlier in the year, he moved to Kansas City, Kansas, where, he recorded in his 1897 autobiography, he "entered a business college of short hand and typewriting." He had hoped to go to work at the "Union telegraph office," but "the thirst for knowledge gained the mastery and I sought to enter Highland College at Highland Kans."[11]

Highland College was a Presbyterian school, founded three years before the Civil War began. Carver applied by mail to attend and was accepted, sight unseen. No doubt he thought that his strong academic credentials and his membership in the Presbyterian church had been the determining factors in his acceptance. But when he arrived on campus to enroll for classes, college officials hastened to correct their "mistake," assuring him that Highland College did not and would not accept "colored" students. For his part, Carver simply recorded that he "was refused on account of my color."[12]

The Highland College rejection was hard on Carver. His impulse seems to have been to leave town quickly, much as he had done in the wake of the Fort Scott lynching. But where was he to go? He had no prospects elsewhere and no funds with which to finance a move, even if he had had a place to go.

Consequently, George remained for some months in Highland, Kansas, perhaps as long as a year. He probably left Highland in the late summer of 1886, at the age of 21 or 22, encouraged by the white family for whom he worked to follow their son, Frank Beeler, to western Kansas, where land was available for homesteading.[13]

Carver arrived in Eden Township, Lane County, Kansas, in mid-August 1886. His arrival was noted in the *Ness County News*. He went to live with and work for a white man named George Steely, with whom he boarded until the following spring.

Carver apparently worked for Steely as both a house and a field hand, helping to erect a house, barn, and outbuildings, while also performing domestic chores. In time, he laid claim to a quarter section of land for himself, built his own sod house, and tried his hand at raising a variety of crops, including "corn, rice corn and a good garden" in the arid Kansas soil. He apparently began to live on his farm on April 20, 1887, two days after completing his house.[14]

Carver's sod house measured 14 x 14 feet and had one window and one door. He placed the value of it at $50 and described the improvements he made to his property as follows: "Breaking 17 acres, value $50; Eight-hundred forest trees, value $200; Fruit trees, $50; Mulberries, Plums, Apricots, value $25; Shrubbery, $10; Total, $325." He also indicated that his house was furnished with "a cook stove and fixtures, Bedstead and beds, cupboard, chairs, table, wash tub and board, and flat irons." The paucity of Carver's possessions notwithstanding, one of his contemporaries remembered years later that Carver took great pains to beautify his home, something he would encourage black Southerners to do as well some years later: "It was so neat, clean and decorated with flowers and objects of interest that no other soddy in the county could compare with it."[15]

Apparently Carver borrowed implements from Mr. Steely to break the prairie ground. His "complete inventory" of farm implements that he owned consisted of "a spade, hoe, and corn planter." Likewise, he indicated that he could afford no livestock, other than "ten hens." Despite digging for water in four different places, he failed to find a water source. Years later, a former neighbor of Carver's remembered the plot of land homesteaded by the future scientist. He told a reporter from the *Kansas City Times* simply, "The land was not very good."[16] To add to Carver's difficulties, his attempt to homestead coincided with one of the worst periods of drought and one of the harshest winters in Kansas history.[17]

Little wonder that Carver was unable to make a living as a Kansas prairie farmer. And yet he appears to have taken with him warm memories of his time in Ness County. For one thing, he seems to have been well liked in the community and to have participated fully in its social life. He participated in and was elected an officer of a local literary society, reading poetry he had written, for example, and participating in musical and theatrical productions. Years later, he expressed appreciation for the opportunities that had been given him in Ness County. Writing to O.L. Lennen, a Ness County official, in 1942, Carver expressed gratitude that Ness Countians had been able "to look into the future of a struggling young Negro boy and discern that there was something in him worthy of a chance in life like other folks." To Knox Barnd, editor of the *Ness County News*, Carver indicated in a letter, "I want to say . . . to the good people of Ness City that I owe much to them for what little I have been able to accomplish, as I do not recall a single instance in which I was not given an opportunity to develop the best that was in me."[18]

Among Carver's talents that seem to have blossomed during his Ness County years was that of painting. Exactly where and when he developed his artistic interests and skills remains unclear. Rackham Holt, whose biography of Carver was reviewed by Carver before his death, recorded that, as a young boy, George wandered into the parlor of a neighbor's house in Diamond, Missouri, and saw portraits of family members hanging on the walls. Holt reported that it was the first time that George saw original art work. "After that," according to Holt, "he was always drawing." In Ness County, Carver encountered his first art teacher, an African American homesteader named Clara M. Duncan, who had previously taught art at Talladega College in Alabama.[19]

Carver's skills as an artist caught the attention of his Ness County, Kansas, neighbors and were reported on in the local newspaper. A rather remarkable biographical sketch of the young would-be sodbuster appeared in the *Ness County News* on March 31, 1888, at a time when Carver was moving into his mid-twenties, still far removed from the fame he would gain as a scientist a generation or more later. One wonders what he had really accomplished by 1888 that prompted the newspaper biographer to take note of him. Like virtually all of the Carver biographies after, the story not only chronicled Carver's accomplishments but emphasized his rise from slavery and, by implication, the distance he had put between himself and the black masses by virtue of his talent and hard work. With regard to his artistry, the writer of the article noted, "He has a fair knowledge of painting, and some of his sketches have considerable merit." The writer added an acknowledgment of the prevalence of racial bias, asserting, "[Carver] is a pleasant and intelligent man to talk with, and were it not for his dusky skin—no fault of his—he might occupy a different sphere to which his ability would otherwise entitle him."[20]

Carver's inability to make a living off of his Kansas prairie farm again set him to wandering. Eventually, his restless search for a better life took him to Winterset, Iowa, probably in 1888 or 1889, although there is at least some evidence that he hoped to return to his Kansas farm when his fortunes improved. Winterset was overwhelmingly white; indeed, the entire state of Iowa had fewer than 11,000 African Americans out of a total population of nearly 2 million residents in 1890.[21]

Carver initially found a job as a cook at Winterset's St. Nicholas Hotel and decided to attend a local white church. As he remembered the experience some 30 years later, he "set [sic] in the rear of the church." The following day, "a handsome man" called for him at the hotel where he was working and living, sent by the man's wife, who wanted to invite Carver into the couple's home.[22]

The couple turned out to be Dr. John and Helen Milholland, he an Ohio-born physician in his mid-forties, she a New York-born housewife in her late thirties. The couple had three daughters and had moved from Ohio to Iowa during the mid-1870s.

Upon arriving at the Milholland home, Carver immediately recognized Helen as "the prima do[n]na in the choir." Mrs. Milholland told Carver his "fine voice" had caused her to notice him, and she asked him "to sing quite a number of pieces for her."

Mrs. Milholland also urged Carver to visit her weekly. "It was her custom," George later remembered, "to have me come . . . and rehearse to her the doings of the day." These encounters with the Milhollands blossomed into a friendship that lasted a lifetime.[23]

Carver opened his heart and soul to the Milhollands. He told them of his travails but also of his dreams and aspirations. He not only sang and performed musically for them but also showed them his needlework and paintings. They became enamored of him, recognized his "specialness," and treated him like a member of the family. "From that time till now," Carver wrote in 1922, "Mr. and Mrs. Milholland have been my warmest and most helpful friends."[24]

Mrs. Milholland especially encouraged Carver in his art work, and she and her husband tried to persuade him to enroll as an art student at Simpson College, a Methodist school in nearby Indianola, Iowa. George was reluctant to try again, fearful that the Highland College experience would be replicated in Iowa. But the Milhollands persisted, promising George to help with the process. Eventually he relented, made application to Simpson College, and was delighted to learn of his acceptance.

In his 1922 reminiscence, Carver recalled that he remained in Winterset for about a year, working and saving money for college expenses before enrolling at Simpson College, where, he remembered, he "took art, music and college work." Once again relying on skills he had learned as a child, he opened a laundry to earn money to sustain himself. "After all my matriculation fees had been paid [a total of $12]," he recalled, "I had 10 c [sic] worth of corn meal, and the other 5 c I spent for beef suet. I lived on these two things one whole week [in his 1897 autobiography, he said it was a whole month]—it took that long for the people to learn that I wanted clothes to wash. After that week I had many friends and plenty of work."[25]

In 1956, Carver's fellow Simpson College student, John P. Morley, recalled what a stir Carver's presence made on the campus when he arrived in September 1890 and how his race worked to his advantage. As Morley recalled, "As he was the only Negro who had ever enrolled at our College, he was the center of interest to the student body." Morley added, "like many of the other students, I was anxious to meet him and form his acquaintance."[26]

Morley "sought him out in the little shack which he had been permitted to occupy rent free." Morley and others who visited Carver noticed that he had no furniture, "so we sat on boxes the merchants of the town had permitted him to take." Eventually, he and others who visited Carver and took their laundry to him felt sorry for him and decided to help him: "a collection was taken among the boys with which to provide him an outfit of table, chairs, and bed." According to Morley, this furniture was "slipped in" to Carver's quarters while he was away because everyone was aware of Carver's independent spirit and did not want to violate it or embarrass George. Years later, in an interview with the Simpson College president, Carver remembered that students sometimes also left him money anonymously: "I often came home and found 25 cents or 50 cents under my door. I would

As a young man, the prepossessing Carver won the attention of several white educators and patrons who became his lifelong friends and supporters. (Courtesy of the Tuskegee University Archives)

not have the slightest idea who put it there."[27] Carver acknowledged the warmth of his reception among the students, writing to Mrs. Milholland, "The people are very kind to me here, and the students are wonderfully good." Years later, he remembered simply, "They made me believe I was a real human being."[28]

Simpson College catalogs for the early 1890s confirm Carver's recollection of the program of study he was enrolled in. He is listed as taking "Select Preparatory" classes as well as courses in voice, piano, and art. According to Carver biographer Linda O. McMurry, Carver's art teacher, Miss Etta Budd, "was at first dubious of both Carver's artistic abilities and his acceptability to the other students in the all-female art department," but, as was so often the case with Carver, he eventually won her over with a combination of his talent, pleasing personality, persistence, and ambition. Soon Professor Budd became one of Carver's strongest supporters and greatest admirers.[29]

While Professor Budd nurtured Carver's growth as an artist, she apparently worried about whether a black man could make a living as an artist. Upon learning of his interest in plants, she suggested that he transfer to Iowa State College at Ames, where her father taught horticulture. Years later, Carver acknowledged that he was persuaded "by my art teacher, Miss Etta M. Budd," to "take a course in Agriculture" at Iowa State, adding, "I am greatly indebted [to her] for whatever measure of success that has come to me."[30]

Carver was ambivalent about leaving Simpson College. He had been wandering for more than a decade, and he had finally found a place and people who satisfied his cravings for friendship, acceptance, educational opportunity, and a chance to pursue his love of art. Years later, he wrote to a friend, "I owe to Simpson College my real beginning of life. . . . [Simpson was] where I got my start, or the beginning of the inspiration to do what the Great Creator in His wisdom has empowered me to do."[31] But he had also begun to think about his future and the work he might engage in once his formal education was finished. He did not want to do other people's laundry for the remainder of his life. And, apparently, he was developing a social conscience that caused him to wonder what he might be able to do to help his people, other African Americans, the vast majority of whom remained mired in economic dependency in the South. Perhaps the study of scientific agriculture would help him to prepare for a career in which he could do well for himself while doing good for others.

His ambivalence about leaving Simpson College was reflected in a letter that he wrote to John and Helen Milholland on August 6, 1891, soon after he arrived on the Iowa State College campus. He told the Milhollands, "I as yet do not like it as well here as I do at S[impson]." He complained rather vaguely that "the helpfull [sic] means for a Christian growth is not so good." And yet, he seemed to understand that Ames was where he needed to be. He was eager to begin his life's work, commenting, "I am so anxious to get out and be doing something. . . . The more my ideas develop, the more beautifull [sic] and grand seems the plan I have laid out to pursue, or rather the one God has destined for me." He commented further, "I seen by one of the late southern papers that one of their strongest men advocates a broader system of education, and lays down a plan very much like the one I have but not as broad."[32]

Was this last comment an oblique reference to Booker T. Washington and his Tuskegee Institute, only recently established in Alabama? Whether or not it was, Carver was clearly developing a sense of mission that prompted him to feel a need to minister to the downtrodden black masses in the South, although he realized that he needed more formal education before he could begin the work that God had chosen him to do.

So, once again, Carver found himself in a new Midwestern town, this time in Ames, Iowa, some 55 miles away, where he enrolled in 1891 as a student at Iowa State College. Initially, it appears as though the school made no provision for lodging for him, the only black student on the campus. Carver referred to this situation in his typically understated way when he wrote about it some years later: "Being a colored boy, and the crowded condition of the school, made it rather embarrassing for some, and it made the question of a room rather puzzling."[33]

Soon, however, the housing problem was solved when Professor James Wilson, a future U.S. Secretary of Agriculture, arranged to house Carver in a room in an empty office. Over the next six years, Carver became a fixture on the campus and achieved a level of happiness that he had not experienced before and, arguably, would never experience again. Carver summed up his time at Iowa State in a letter: "I did odd jobs of all kinds for [a] number of the professors; such as cutting wood, making gardens; working in the fields; helping clean house; taking care of the green house and the chemical, botanical and bacteriological laboratories."[34] He had a place and a purpose, preparing, as he was, for a future that was still taking shape.

NOTES

1. Rackham Holt, *George Washington Carver: An American Biography*, rev. ed. (Garden City, NY: Doubleday, 1943), 39–40. Details about the Payne family and demographic figures for the Fort Scott

population are derived from federal census records, available through Ancestry.com.

2. Linda O. McMurry, *George Washington Carver: Scientist and Symbol* (New York: Oxford University Press, 1981), 22–23; Carver quoted in Gary R. Kremer, ed., *George Washington Carver: In His Own Words* (Columbia: University of Missouri Press, 1987), 149.

3. Robert P. Fuller and Merrill J. Mattes, "The Early Life of George Washington Carver," unpublished manuscript, George Washington Carver National Monument, Diamond, Missouri, November 1957, 57.

4. McMurry, *George Washington Carver*, 23.

5. Federal census records may be accessed through Ancestry.com

6. Ibid., 23–24; Rarig quoted in Fuller and Mattes, "The Early Life of George Washington Carver," 62–63.

7. Fuller and Mattes, "The Early Life of George Washington Carver," 61, 63; Kremer, *George Washington Carver*, 23–24.

8. Fuller and Mattes, "The Early Life of George Washington Carver," 61, 63.

9. Fuller and Mattes, "The Early Life of George Washington Carver," 60; Holt, *George Washington Carver*, 50.

10. Kremer, *George Washington Carver*, 24.

11. Ibid., 21.

12. Ibid.

13. Fuller and Mattes, "The Early Life of George Washington Carver," 65–67.

14. Ibid., 71–86.

15. O. L. Lennen, quoted in Mark D. Hersey, "'My Work Is That of Conservation': The Environmental Vision of George Washington Carver," Ph.D. diss., University of Kansas, 2006, 40–60.

16. Quoted in Hersey, "'My Work Is That of Conservation,'" 41.

17. Hersey, "'My Work Is That of Conservation,'" 41.

18. Quoted in Kremer, *George Washington Carver*, 42–43.

19. McMurry, *George Washington Carver*, 26.

20. *Ness County News*, March 31, 1888, quoted in Fuller and Mattes, "The Early Life of George Washington Carver," 72.

21. Demographic data gleaned from federal census returns, available from Ancestry.com.

22. Kremer, *George Washington Carver*, 24.

23. Ibid.

24. Ibid.

25. Ibid.

26. Morley's comment notwithstanding, at least one other African American had attended Simpson College prior to Carver's enrollment there. Fuller and Mattes, "The Early Life of George Washington Carver," 90.

27. Quoted in Hersey, "'My Work Is That of Conservation,'" 47.

28. Ibid.

29. McMurry, *George Washington Carver*, 31.

30. Kremer, *George Washington Carver*, 50.

31. Quoted in Hersey, "'My Work Is That of Conservation,'" 49–90.

32. Kremer, *George Washington Carver*, 45–46.

33. Fuller and Mattes, "The Early Life of George Washington Carver," 93.

34. Ibid.

Chapter 3

THE IOWA STATE YEARS

[H]e is by all means the ablest student we have here.

—James Wilson, letter to unspecified officials of Alcorn
Agricultural and Mechanical College, Mississippi

George Washington Carver's decision to enroll as a student of scientific agriculture at Iowa State College during the early 1890s was a pragmatic one, made just as the philosophical movement known as "pragmatism" began to gain widespread acceptance throughout industrializing America. No evidence exists that Carver had read works by famous pragmatic philosophers such as the Harvard-educated Charles Sanders Peirce, Harvard's William James, or the University of Chicago's John Dewey, but his decision to go to Ames, Iowa, was shaped by ideas that each man would have shared: a belief in the rights and opportunities of democracy; faith in science as an instrument of progress; and, a commitment to using new found knowledge for the good of mankind.

Carver could not have chosen a better place to go to pursue a practical education in agriculture. During the early 1890s, Iowa State College emerged as the leading institution in the country where students could focus on "scientific agriculture," a field of study that promoted the use of scientific research and experimentation to improve the quality and quantity of America's food supply. The effort was headed by James Wilson, a Scottish immigrant, former Iowa legislator, and former U.S. congressman, who had served on the Committee on Agriculture as a U.S. Representative. Wilson arrived at Ames in the fall of 1891 to serve as a professor of agriculture and director of the Experiment Station.[1]

Carver, too, arrived on the Iowa State College campus in the fall of 1891 and almost immediately became close friends with Professor Wilson. Already in his mid-twenties and somewhat older than most of his fellow students, Carver evidenced a seriousness of purpose that bespoke not only his age but also his life experiences and a conviction that God was preparing him for some great work among his own people.

Carver faced challenges as the only African American on campus. Indeed, as one of his contemporaries remembered it, he was not only the lone black student at Iowa State College, he was "the only colored boy . . . in Ames."[2] At times, especially early on, he endured derision, ostracism, and overt hostility because of his race. At times, also, he was able to turn his race to his advantage, calling attention indirectly to the obstacles he faced and the disadvantages he encountered, evoking a desire in white faculty members and fellow students to help him in a variety of ways. In the end, the black Carver almost always won over his white critics.

According to Carver biographer Linda McMurray, hostility toward Carver on account of his race surfaced the first day he set foot on campus when "a group of boys shouted derogatory names at him."[3] Additionally, as noted in the previous chapter, he had no place to stay. Years later, Carver's mentor, the botanist Louis Hermann Pammel, remembered that he and Professor and Mrs. James Wilson tried to find lodging for Carver in a private home. The people they contacted, however, expressed a fondness for Carver, "but owing to the fact that he was a colored boy they all said they would not like to have him in the house."[4] Left unstated was an explanation of why Professor Pammel or the Wilsons did not open their homes to Carver.

To make matters worse, the manager of the dining room required Carver to take his meals with the wait staff and other menial workers at the university. Carver apparently wrote a letter explaining these circumstances to an old friend in Indianola, Iowa, Mrs. Sophia Liston, whose husband, William, operated a bookstore there. Mrs. Liston had befriended Carver during his years in Indianola. Indeed, there are at least some reports that he lived briefly with the Listons, that he often came to their house to study, and that he and Mrs. Liston painted and worked together in her garden.[5]

In an illustration of the kind of intense loyalty Carver elicited from his close friends and the kind of protectiveness they exhibited toward and over him, Mrs. Liston responded to Carver's letter of distress by taking immediate and direct action. She recalled some years later, "I immediately put on my best dress and hat and took the train for Ames," a distance of more than 70 miles. Upon arriving at Iowa State College, the white Mrs. Liston, who signed her letters to Carver "your mother," made a point of dining with Carver in his segregated dining spot and then walked all over campus with him in an extraordinary gesture of fearless friendship. This act on Mrs. Liston's part paved the way for others to befriend the future scientist. As Carver later reported to Mrs. Liston, "The next day, everything was different, the ice was broken, and from that [moment] on, things went very much easier."[6]

George Washington Carver soon settled in to the rhythm of academic life and was apparently a good student who excelled in botany, did slightly better than average in other classes, including chemistry, and harbored a dislike of history and geometry. Like all undergraduates at Iowa State, Carver participated in military classes, excelling as a student cadet and rising to the rank of cadet captain.[7] His seemingly complete integration into the life of the campus is best illustrated by his involvement in a wide range of extracurricular activities.

Carver seems to have been a joiner, belonging to so many groups that one is tempted to say that he craved attention and acceptance. Early in his tenure at Iowa State, he helped to organize a student prayer group, and later he became involved with the campus Young Men's Christian Association (YMCA). Professor Wilson, the faculty member who provided a room for Carver early on, was a deeply religious man who hosted a Bible study class and worked closely with Carver. Years later, Wilson remembered, "when students began coming in at the beginning of a new term, Carver and I would sit down and plan how to get boys who were Christian to go down to the depot to meet them, come up with them and help them get registered, help them get rooms, and all that which would establish acquaintance with them and enable young men of Christian leanings to get into prayer meetings, etc."[8]

Carver's work with the YMCA led to his being chosen to serve as missionary chairman for the campus organization. During his junior and senior years at Iowa State, he was selected to represent the college at YMCA summer camps at Lake Geneva, Wisconsin. Carver seemed to enjoy these camps and participated fully in activities, from croquet to water sports. He also led "collecting" forays around the camp, identifying and gathering plants native to the region. Although a majority of the youths involved in the camp seemed to be unbothered by the presence of an African American among them, years later, one of the attendees, Willis D. Weatherford, admitted, "those of us from the South thought it a little queer that there should be a Negro delegate present."[9]

In addition to these activities, Carver also joined the Welch Eclectic Society, an organization that promoted the study of science, literature, and the art of public speaking.

His name appeared frequently in the *Iowa Agricultural Student*, a weekly campus newspaper, in conjunction with stories about Welch Society events. Once, for example, the organization held a musical program that included a "recitation" titled "How Rubenstein Played," performed by Carver. On another occasion, he joined another student in "a violin and guitar duet."[10]

Yet another organization Carver belonged to was the Agricultural Society. His skill as an artist led members of the Welsh Eclectic Society and the Agricultural Society to enlist him to decorate halls and other meeting rooms where the groups gathered for formal events.

Carver also continued painting while at Iowa State. Indeed, he returned to Indianola during his first extended break from classes at Iowa State College to enroll in an art class with Miss Etta Budd at Simpson.[11] During late December 1892, an exhibition of work by Iowa artists was held in Davenport, Iowa, approximately 200 miles from Ames. Professors James Wilson and Louis H. Pammell, along with a number of Carver's fellow students, were eager to see Carver travel to Davenport and enter at least some of his art work into this competition. Knowing that Carver could not afford the cost of transportation, group members purchased a railroad ticket for him. Then, apparently, the group "tricked" him into trying on a new suit, shoes, hat, and gloves in a men's clothing store. Subsequently, they purchased the new wardrobe for Carver and presented it to him.[12]

Carver entered four paintings in the competition, all of them of flowers. According to Carver biographer, Rackham Holt, exhibition judges chose all of Carver's paintings to represent Iowa art at the 1893 World's Columbian Exhibition, held in Chicago. Carver, however, sent only one of the four, a painting of a Yucca plant.[13] Still, having the quality of his work validated by independent judges was immensely satisfying to him. In subsequent years, he remembered the experience fondly and commented on it on more than one occasion in his correspondence with James Wilson and Louis H. Pammel. Some 30 years after the event, Carver wrote to Pammel, telling him, "you may be surprised to know that I wore the suit you fooled me into the store and bought for me while in school, I wore it to a banquet, suit, hat and gloves, the people thought it new."[14]

In addition to all of these activities, plus his normal coursework, Carver managed to make at least one scholarly presentation at the annual meeting of the Iowa Horticultural Society and to publish an article, "Grafting the Cacti," in that organization's official publication. It is worth noting, as historian Mark Hersey has pointed out, that one can see present in this early writing a theme that Carver would repeat time and again throughout his career: that nothing in nature exists without purpose and that there was no such thing as waste: "Those who have given [cacti] little or no thought are apt to judge too harshly concerning their merits and demerits . . . nature does not expend its forces upon waste material, but that each created thing is an indispensable factor in the great whole, and one in which no other factor will fit exactly as well."[15]

Carver's undergraduate degree program required that he write a thesis. His work, "Plants as Modified by Man," described experiments he and others had done grafting and crossbreeding a number of plants. In his undergraduate thesis, carried out under the direction and with the encouragement of Etta Budd's father, Joseph, Carver explored and embraced ideas that informed his work for the remainder of his life. He paid homage to Charles Darwin and to "the excellent work of [Luther]

Burbank," the California botanist and horticulturalist whose cross-breeding experiments with plants, begun during the late 19th century, were aimed at improving the quality and quantity of the world's food supply. "Man," Carver asserted, "is simply nature's agent or employee," whose challenge is "to assist [nature] in her work." Scientific experimentation, Carver believed, could serve "as an aid to nature in carrying out her plans methodically, instead of at random[,] as is the case when left to herself to perform the work." Given this belief, Carver asked rhetorically in the concluding paragraph of his thesis, "Why should not the horticulturist know just how to build up size, flavor, vigor and hardiness in his fruits and shrubs, and the florist know just how to proceed to unite, blende [sic] and perfect the color of his flowers, producing not only harmony, but a glorious symphony of nature's daintiest tints and shades, with just as much certainty as the artist mixes his pigments upon the palette?"[16]

Apart from his academic work and the tasks he took on for income that allowed him to pay his own way, Carver seems to have been in demand as a public speaker away from campus. The Iowa State student newspaper noted in March 1896 that Carver gave "a series of lectures on Flora culture" in Mediapolis, nearly 200 miles from Ames. The next month, he addressed a "Sunday School convention at Ontario," just a few miles from Ames, on the topic "Sabbath School Normal Class." In May 1896, he delivered an address in Cambridge, Iowa, approximately 17 miles from Ames. Clearly, he was known not only on the campus but off the campus, as well.[17]

Carver's success as an undergraduate student led to multiple rewards and opportunities at Iowa State. In October 1894, just weeks before his graduation from Iowa State College, Carver wrote his old Winterset friends, the Milhollands, telling them, "The Lord is wonderfully blessing me and has for these many years. I have been elected assistant station botanist [sic]. I intend to take a post graduate course here, which will take two years."[18] Carver was given a paid position in the botany department, a job that placed him in charge of the college's greenhouse. As Linda McMurry has pointed out, this allowed Carver for the first time to avoid the drudgery of menial jobs to pay his way as a student.[19] By this time, he was no longer living in an abandoned office.

Instead, he and two other students boarded with Professor Eliza Owens, who taught domestic economy at Iowa State College. The 1895 Iowa State College yearbook described Carver as "Gifted with an intense love of nature, he is an artist of the most delicate touch and is also an earnest conscentious [sic] Christian worker."[20]

As a graduate student, Carver worked under the tutelage of Louis H. Pammel, a Wisconsin-born son of German immigrants who arrived at Iowa State College in the spring of 1889 to teach botany. Pammel was only two years older than his prized student. Carver specialized in plant pathology and mycology and earned Pammel's praise. Pammel referred to him as "the best collector I ever had in the department or have ever known." While a graduate student at Iowa State, Carver coauthored three articles on mycology, two of them with Professor Pammel.[21]

As was so often the case with Carver, he developed a deep personal relationship with his mentor, Pammel, that manifested itself in a multiplicity of ways. In the early 1920s, when fame and notoriety began to come his way, Carver passed on the praise to Pammel, telling him, "God evidently arranged it so that I should fall into your hands for training and I am simply carrying out in my poor way just the things you endeavored so earnestly and patiently to teach me."[22] When Pammel retired, in 1924, Carver wrote him a letter of appreciation, thanking him "for the very personal interest you took in me," adding, "whatever success I have been able to attain is due, in very large measure, to you, my beloved teacher, Christian gentleman, and friend."[23]

Carver not only developed a close friendship with Pammel, he also became friends with Pammel's wife and the couple's children. A quarter-century after he left Iowa State, Carver continued to correspond with multiple Pammel family members, and, in 1931, two of the couple's daughters visited him at Tuskegee after their father's death.[24]

In addition to working with Pammel, Carver's graduate school responsibilities included teaching freshmen biology courses. As a teacher, Carver was widely popular with his students and evidenced a strong commitment to the Socratic method, forcing his students to work for answers and responding to their queries with questions that forced them to think more deeply. It was an approach to teaching that he continued to use throughout his life.[25]

By 1896, Carver had been a promising Iowa State College student for half a decade. As he moved toward the completion of his graduate work, he and others wondered where the promise would lead. Many in the Iowa State family wanted him to remain at the school, and there is abundant evidence that school officials would have made a place for him. His reputation as a researcher, teacher, and collegial coworker guaranteed him a place at Iowa State College as long as he wanted to stay there.

Carver retained, however, the commitment to serving the downtrodden of his race that had prompted him to go to Ames to begin with. Already in the fall of 1895, a full year before receiving his master's degree, Carver received word of a possible job offer from Alcorn Agricultural and Mechanical College in Mississippi. This was a state-supported school for African Americans, whose first president was Hiram Revels, one of two black politicians to represent Mississippi in the U.S. Senate during Reconstruction. Carver went so far as to provide administrators of Alcorn with letters of recommendation, endorsing him as a suitable candidate for the job. Indeed, the letters reflected a benevolent protectionism of Carver that seemed to evidence not only strong support for his qualifications but also a genuine concern for his future well-being and a reluctance to allow him to leave.

Iowa State College president William Miller Beardshear wrote that Carver was "universally liked by faculty and students" and emphasized, "We would not care to have him change unless he can better himself." Professors Budd and Pammel praised Carver also, with Pammel predicting, "Mr. Carver has a great future before him." Neither man wanted Carver to leave Iowa State. James Wilson was the most effusive in his praise. He wrote that, "in cross-fertilization . . . and the propagation of plants, he is by all means the ablest student we have here" and asserted, "We have nobody to take his place." Wilson added, "it will be difficult, in fact impossible, to fill his place," adding, "I would never part with a student with so much regret as George Carver." Aware that his praise was unusually flattering, Wilson concluded, "[words] such as [these] I have never before spoken in favor of any young man leaving our institution, but they are all deserved."[26]

In the end, Carver declined the Alcorn offer or at least postponed accepting it until he was closer to finishing his graduate degree. In the spring of 1896, just as he was about to complete his formal education and begin the real life work for which his studies had prepared him, Carver began to be recruited by Booker T. Washington, who was looking for someone to lead the newly created Agricultural Department at Tuskegee Institute in Alabama.

A decade older than Carver and with a clear and real memory of slavery, Washington had established Tuskegee as an educational institution for a generation of African Americans who had been born during the immediate post–Civil War period. Opened in 1881 and supported by wealthy whites, Tuskegee Institute was a place where black youths could learn practical skills that would allow them to earn a living, whether as farmers or as skilled artisans.[27]

In 1895, Washington laid out his philosophy of "accommodation" in a speech delivered at the Atlanta Exposition to a mixed-race audience. African Americans, Washington asserted, should gain economic independence before seeking social and political equality. They should "cast down their buckets" where they were, learn to support themselves and their families, and accept the South's racial caste system until they had proven themselves worthy of social uplift.[28]

Washington, of course, had his critics, the most famous of whom was the brilliant African American scholar W.E.B. DuBois, the first black person to earn a Ph.D. from Harvard University. DuBois condemned Washington's unwillingness to challenge white racism and proposed, instead, that African Americans demand political and social equality with whites as part of their birthright as American citizens. Carver, the man who was raised by whites and who had benefited from white beneficence at virtually every stage of his life, was much more inclined to agree with Washington's approach than with that of DuBois. Indeed, in May 1896, Carver wrote to Washington, telling him, "I read your stirring address delivered at Chicago and I said amen to all you said," adding, "you have the correct solution to the 'race problem.'"[29]

Washington had learned of Carver, his interests and abilities, early in 1896. Aware of the reputation of Iowa State College in the area of agriculture, Washington wrote to Iowa State president Beardshear in search of a "colored graduate" of the school. President Beardshear responded on March 6, 1896, telling Washington about Carver, whom he described as "a thorough christian gentleman and scholar." Beardshear assured Washington of Carver's worthiness for a job at Tuskegee: "We

can give him iron-clad recommendations. Any school would be fortunate in securing his services."[30]

Soon after receiving Beardshear's letter, Washington began his active recruitment of Carver, writing to him to inquire as to his interest
in joining the Tuskegee Institute faculty and heading the soon-to-be
established agricultural department. In his letter to Carver, Washington explained, "Tuskegee Institute seeks to provide education—a
means for survival to those who attend. Our students are poor, often
starving. They travel miles of torn roads, across years of poverty now.
We teach them to read and write, but words cannot fill stomachs. They
need to learn how to plant and harvest crops." Washington continued,
"I cannot offer you money, position or fame. The first two you have.
The last, from the place you occupy, you will no doubt achieve. These
things I now ask you to give up. I offer you in their place—work—hard
work—the challenge of bringing people from degradation, poverty and
waste to full manhood."[31]

Carver's response to Washington's eloquent plea was delayed until
April 3, 1896; he had, he wrote, been away on "a lecture tour." Carver's
response was cagey; he clearly wanted to play hard to get. He sought
to let Washington know that he was about to earn a master's degree in
agriculture and that he was happy at Iowa State, commenting, "I hardly
think I desire to make a change." He did inform Washington that
"I expect to take up work amongst my people" and flattered Washington by telling him, "[I] have known of and appreciate the great work
you are doing." He also told Washington of the offer to join the faculty
of Alcorn Agricultural and Mechanical College.[32]

Carver was not as dead set against going to Tuskegee as his letter to
Washington implied. After telling Washington that he did not want to
leave Iowa State and that he already had a job offer in Mississippi, he
penned a postscript, telling the Alabamian, "Should you think further
on this matter I can furnish you with all the recommendations you will
care to look over."

Two days after sending this letter to Washington, Carver apparently
began to fear that his attempt to let Washington know that he had
options other than Tuskegee might have sounded too harsh. He wrote
again, this time reaffirming his desire to remain at Iowa State but let-

ting Washington know he "might be induced to leave" if a "satisfactory position" was offered him.[33]

Again Washington wrote to Carver, trying to persuade him to come to Tuskegee. Again Carver responded with a combination of comments asserting that he had other offers and encouraging Washington to continue courting him. He also assured Washington, "Of course it has always been the one great ideal of my life to be of the greatest good to the greatest number of 'my people' possible," adding, "to this end I have been preparing myself for these many years."[34]

On April 17, 1896, Washington offered Carver a position at Tuskegee, telling him, "we can pay you one thousand dollars . . . a year and board, board to include all expenses except traveling." He flattered Carver by telling him he was the only "colored man" in the country qualified for the job, an important consideration, given Washington's desire to employ an all-black staff. If Carver declined the offer, Washington wrote, "we shall be forced perhaps to put in a white man." Washington also emphasized that he wanted to hire people who wanted to work at Tuskegee to help uplift the race, not just to make money. Still, he assured Carver, "If the terms I have named are not satisfactory we shall be willing to do anything in reason that will enable you to decide in favor of coming to Tuskegee."[35]

Despite Washington's offer of a job to Carver, and despite Carver's assertion that "if I come the money will not be the sole object, only secondary," Carver continued to try to impress Washington with his abilities and his options. He told Washington, "One institution near you offers me the same as you with the understanding that my work is to recommend me an advance in wages[,] also a house." He wrote his letter on Iowa State College letterhead and drew Washington's attention to that fact, telling him, "I already have a position here as you will see by the letter head and one of my professors told me today they would raise my wages here if I would stay."[36]

What was Carver's motive in responding to Washington in such a tentative, ambivalent way? Perhaps he was hoping that Washington would offer him a larger salary, although his April 21 letter to the Tuskegee principal assured Washington that "the financial feature is at present satisfactory."

Booker T. Washington invited Carver to come to Tuskegee Institute in 1896. The two were to have a contentious but productive partnership. (Library of Congress Prints & Photographs Division/LC-USZ62-119898)

More likely, Carver simply wanted to impress Washington, to let Washington know how well qualified he was, how committed he was to "his people," how lucky Washington would be to have Carver on his faculty. Likewise, Carver seemed to want to let Washington know how much of a personal sacrifice he was making in leaving the comfort of an all-white northern school for the challenges and discomfort of a struggling all-black southern institution.

Carver wanted to be needed, perhaps even to be begged. His eagerness to please and to impress people he thought of as authority figures was a constant reality throughout his life, a tendency that led him on occasion to be simultaneously obsequious and boastful. Perhaps the insecurity that lay behind this search for approval stemmed from his childhood as an orphan and his struggles as a black man in a white world.

Whatever the complexity of motives that led Carver to continue trying to impress Booker T. Washington, even after he had accepted the latter's offer of a job, Carver was about to embark on a journey for which, in many ways, he was totally unprepared. Although he sought to live and work among "his people," Carver had, arguably, had little exposure to black southern culture or African American institutions. Indeed, it might be argued that he had been shaped and molded more by white than by black mores and traditions. Nothing that he had experienced in Missouri, Kansas, or Iowa could have prepared him for the predominately black world of Tuskegee Institute that he was about to enter.

NOTES

1. Mark D. Hersey, "'My Work Is That of Conservation': The Environmental Vision of George Washington Carver," Ph.D. diss., University of Kansas, 2006, 50–60.

2. Quoted in ibid., 61.

3. Linda O. McMurry, *George Washington Carver: Scientist and Symbol* (New York: Oxford University Press, 1981), 33.

4. Quoted in Hersey, "'My Work Is That of Conservation,'" 61–62.

5. Ed Carty, *George Washington Carver in Indianola: A Tour Guide* (Indianola, IA: Warren County Historical Society, 1990), unpaginated.

6. Quoted in McMurry, *George Washington Carver*, 33.

7. Hersey, "'My Work Is That of Conservation,'" 91–92.

8. Quoted in McMurry, *George Washington Carver*, 34.

9. Rackham Holt, *George Washington Carver: An American Biography*, rev. ed. (Garden City NY: Doubleday, 1943), 91–94, McMurry, *George Washington Carver*, 35.

10. Robert P. Fuller and Merrill J. Mattes, "The Early Life of George Washington Carver," unpublished manuscript, George Washington Carver National Monument, Diamond, Missouri, November 1957, "Exhibit N," unpaginated.

11. Hersey, "'My Work Is That of Conservation,'" 62.

12. Holt, *George Washington Carver*, 95–96.

13. Ibid., 97.

14. Quoted in Gary R. Kremer, ed., *George Washington Carver: In His Own Words* (Columbia: University of Missouri Press, 1987), 55.

15. Quoted in Hersey, "'My Work Is That of Conservation,'" 92, 93.

16. George Washington Carver, "Plants as Modified by Man," B.S. thesis, George Washington Carver Papers, Iowa State University Archives, 2–3; also quoted in Hersey, "'My Work Is That of Conservation,'" 93–94.

17. Fuller and Mattis, "Exhibit N," unpaginated.

18. Quoted in Kremer, *George Washington Carver*, 46.

19. McMurry, *George Washington Carver*, 39.

20. Quoted in Hersey, "'My Work Is That of Conservation,'" 96.

21. McMurry, *George Washington Carver*, 39–41.

22. Quoted in Hersey, "'My Work Is That of Conservation,'" 79.

23. Quoted in Kremer, *George Washington Carver*, 56.

24. Kremer, *George Washington Carver*, 58–59.

25. McMurry, *George Washington Carver*, 40.

26. Quoted in Hersey, "'My Work Is That of Conservation,'" 98–99.

27. For the most recent biography of Booker T. Washington, see Robert J. Norrell, *Up from History: The Life of Booker T. Washington* (Cambridge, MA: Harvard University Press, 2009).

28. Ibid., 121–28.

29. Quoted in Kremer, *George Washington Carver*, 63–64.

30. Louis R. Harlan, ed., *The Booker T. Washington Papers*, vol. 4: 1896–1898 (Urbana: University of Illinois Press, 1975), 126.

31. Quoted in William J. Federer, *George Washington Carver: His Life and Faith in His Own Words* (St. Louis, MO: Amerisearch, 2002), 14.

32. Quoted in Kremer, *George Washington Carver*, 61.

33. Ibid., 61–62.

34. Ibid., 62.

35. Harlan, *The Booker T. Washington Papers*, vol. 4, 162.

36. Quoted in Kremer, *George Washington Carver*, 63.

Chapter 4

TROUBLE AT TUSKEGEE

In a strange land among a strange people.

—George Washington Carver, "A Gleam upon the Distant Horizon"

Carver biographer Linda McMurry has observed that George Washington Carver arrived on the Tuskegee campus in 1896 likely feeling "invincible."[1] He was the only African American in the country who had earned a graduate degree in agriculture. Indeed, as a coworker remembered years later, "He was the first one on the [Tuskegee Institute] faculty to have a master's degree." This colleague remembered also, "Some of his detractors, I suppose, would say he did not let people forget it."[2] No other Tuskegee faculty member had attended a northern, white school. Instead, most had been trained at Hampton Normal and Agricultural Institute in Virginia, the alma mater of Tuskegee's principal, Booker T. Washington.

Carver had been courted heavily by Washington and had persuaded Washington to pay him $1,000 per year to head up Tuskegee's Agricultural Department, a position that included teaching responsibilities, doing research, and managing the school's farm. In his autobiography,

Washington praised Carver as "a thoroughly educated man in all matters pertaining to agriculture."[3]

But Carver's feeling of invincibility led to a thinly veiled arrogance and a propensity to make demands, both of which angered and alienated many of the people he encountered. In a sense, Carver traveled to Tuskegee as something of a missionary to southern blacks, a people who seemed somewhat foreign to him and toward whom he felt superior. As he wrote some years later, upon arriving at Tuskegee, he felt like he was "in a strange land among a strange people."[4] Like many other missionaries traveling to "foreign" lands before and since, Carver expected deference and solicitation from the people he purported to serve. The practice at Tuskegee at the time of Carver's arrival, for example, was that unmarried male instructors lived two to a room. Carver found this arrangement unacceptable; he demanded two rooms—one for himself and another for the multitude of plant specimens he continued to collect.

His demand fell on deaf ears. When Carver did not receive the response he hoped for, he decided to go over Washington's head and appeal directly to the school's finance committee, a gesture that evidenced his ignorance of just how autocratically and totally Washington controlled happenings at the school. There was no higher authority than Booker T. Washington on the Tuskegee Institute campus.

Carver's letter to the "Messrs of the Finance Committee," dated November 27, 1896, only weeks after he had arrived on campus, created a great chasm between himself and Washington, as well as between him and much of the rest of the Tuskegee faculty and staff. Reading the letter today, even after the passage of more than a century, one cannot help but be struck by its author's arrogance, presumptuousness, and plain bad judgment.

Carver began the letter by pointing out "the valuable nature of . . . my collections" and proceeded with what was arguably a less than completely honest assertion that "You doubtless know that I came here solely for the benefit of my people, no other motive in view." Then, in what was clearly the most egregious tactical error in the letter, he announced that he did not intend to stay long at Tuskegee, at least not as a teacher and agriculturalist: "I do not expect to teach many years, but will quit as soon as I can trust my work to others, and engage in my brushwork, which will be of great honor to our people."[5]

Carver simply could not believe that any reasonable person with the authority to honor his request would fail to do so. He complained, "At present I have no rooms to unpack my goods," and added that the failure of school officials to accommodate him handicapped his work and endangered his valuable collection of plant specimens.

It is remarkable that Carver, a man who was so good at getting what he wanted and needed from whites through an obsequious and inoffensive approach, resorted to insensitive and arrogant demands upon people of his own race. One is tempted to believe that Carver accepted many of the prevailing negative stereotypes about African Americans and that he felt superior to most, if not all, of his Tuskegee coworkers.

Apart from his rocky start with Booker T. Washington and many faculty and staff members at Tuskegee, Carver seems to have acclimated to his new environment fairly quickly. In late March 1897, he wrote to Mrs. Louis H. Pammel, the wife of his graduate school mentor, telling her, "I am enjoying my work very much indeed." He described the weather as "simply superb," although he would soon be complaining about the extreme heat of his first Alabama summer. He told Mrs. Pammel of the many flowers that were in bloom and the fruits and vegetables that were already growing. While he found the area "very poor" and a "new world to Iowa," he told Mrs. Pammel, "I like it [at Tuskegee] so much better than I thought I would at first."[6]

Alabama was, indeed, a new world to Carver, unlike any other place he had ever lived. With a population nearly 400,000 fewer people than the state Carver had most recently called home, Alabama had nearly 70 times as many African Americans as Iowa. Macon County, where Tuskegee was located, had nearly four times as many blacks as whites. For Carver, living in a community where blacks outnumbered whites truly was like living in a foreign country.[7]

Carver was correct, also, in his assessment of Alabama as being "very poor." Indeed, the vast majority of black Alabamians were desperately poor. In the 1890s, Alabama had nearly three times as many agricultural workers as Iowa, more than half of them "colored." Additionally, Alabama had roughly 60,000 African American female agricultural workers; Iowa had 407. More than 80 percent of Alabama's "servants" were African American. In Macon County, as historian Mark Hersey has pointed out, "By the close of the 1890s only 157 African Americans owned their own farms," out of a total black population of nearly 19,000. "At the time of Carver's arrival," Hersey continued, "most of Macon County's blacks were tenant farmers of various sorts, many were sharecroppers."[8]

Booker T. Washington's goal was to help these landless, dependent laborers to develop skills that would allow them to establish economic autonomy. He demanded much of everyone associated with Tuskegee, Carver included. Carver was expected to direct the operations of the newly established agricultural Experiment Station, of course, but he was also expected to teach, to do outreach extension work, and to conduct research. And, as if that were not enough, Washington expected Carver to manage all aspects of the school's agricultural operations, to supervise the landscaping of the Institute's grounds, even to oversee the operation of water closets and other sanitation facilities.[9]

Although Carver's decision to take up scientific agriculture had been driven by pragmatism, there was a streak of impractical spontaneity in him. He often evidenced the unpredictable temperament of the artist, who, when the mood struck him, would abandon his normal duties so that he could spend an afternoon doing his "brush work." Indeed, some four and one-half years after arriving on the Tuskegee campus, he wrote to Principal Washington, asking for new living quarters that would include a room in which he could "do some historic painting," adding, "I greatly desire to do this that it may go down in the history of the race."[10] Although no record of Washington's response to this request, if there was one, survives, it seems unlikely that the principal took kindly to the notion of his director of agriculture spending his time painting.

Washington, of course, had no patience with any kind of impetuousness. He was the ultimate pragmatist. In fact, he had no patience for anything that did not result in an immediately measurable benefit to the efficient and productive improvement of the operation of the Institute. He thought Carver was a bad manager of both people and resources. He continuously pushed Carver to do more with less. Carver, in turn, continually asked for more resources and less work.

In May 1898, less than two years after his arrival on campus, Carver wrote a lengthy letter to Washington, outlining his frustrations and threatening to quit if Washington did not do something to remedy them. He began the letter by assuring Washington that "no one is more deeply interested in the welfare of the school than myself" and chronicled how he had worked "early and late and at times beyond my physical strength" for the good of the school.[11]

He tried to explain that he had made personal sacrifices. He had, he wrote, "made partial arrangements to enter the Shaw School of Botany, St. Louis, from which I hope to take my doctor's degree" a degree, he emphasized, "that no colored man has ever taken." Instead, he "canceled [the] engagement with Shaw" because of Washington's "many letters urging the cutting down of expenses, . . . your desire to have me study the food question . . . and the very important relationship the farm as a whole stands to the financial side of the school."

Carver outlined the ways in which he hoped to make the Agricultural Department grow so that it could become "second to none in the U.S. in the matters of equipments, methods of teaching and results obtained." Clearly, he tried to engage Washington in his vision of what he hoped to accomplish, if only he could be given adequate time and resources: "It is impossible for me to do this work without men and means. . . . I simply want a chance to do what I know can be done."[12]

In pointing out his successes, however, Carver felt compelled, also, to call attention to the deficiencies of his coworkers, an action that, no doubt, exacerbated tension between himself and other staff members. Most of all, he bristled at the notion that people whom he regarded as intellectual inferiors would be placed in authority over him and be allowed to second-guess his decisions or criticize his work. "Now Mr. Washington," he somberly stated, "I think it ludicrously unfair to have persons sit in an office and dictate what I have to do and how I can do it." No doubt hoping to prompt Washington to act in his favor, Carver threatened to leave Tuskegee if things did not change. Or, as he put it, "If I thought things were to run as they have always run I would not stay here any longer than I could get away."[13]

Carver's threat to leave notwithstanding, Washington showed no inclination to change his expectations of Carver or the way he treated him, and he also declined to increase significantly the resources he

Carver's spontaneity and playfulness won him the devotion of his students, but his relationships with his colleagues often were strained. Nevertheless, some appreciated his unconventional humor. (Courtesy of the Tuskegee University Archives)

made available to Carver. Moreover, Washington tried to improve Carver's managerial effectiveness by looking over his shoulder at every turn. Indeed, there seemed to be nothing that Carver did that could not be criticized by the principal. In June 1898, for example, Washington wrote Carver a short but stern letter, telling him, "I want the milk report every morning, and on it I want the number of cows milked." On another occasion, some months later, Washington took exception to what he regarded as inappropriate dress among Carver's student workers and addressed him as follows: "Hereafter I wish you would have all persons in your division . . . insist that students wear overalls, and that the young men be prohibited from working in their undershirts as I find some of them are doing."[14] Yet again, Washington complained, "I hope you will give more attention to beautifying and keeping in shape the grounds in front of the poultry yard."[15] Once, in fact, Washington chastised Carver for showing up late to a staff meeting called by his half brother, John H. Washington. Carver responded to the reprimand with no little frustration, pointing out to the principal that he was late because "I was detained by *you in your office*."[16]

Carver responded to criticisms such as these by plodding on with inadequate resources, writing letters of complaint to Washington, and nurturing a growing feeling that he was insufficiently appreciated among a group of people who were not, quite frankly, his peers. Washington even found something to criticize in Carver's means of communication. At one point, with no little exasperation, he wrote to tell Carver, "Unless it is something very important, I wish you to use a cheap grade of paper hereafter in sending notes."[17] Presumably this message was conveyed on "a cheap grade of paper."

Washington did not like anyone questioning his decisions or the authority that allowed him to make them. Once, in complete frustration, he wrote to tell Carver, "I fear that you . . . are inclined to misinterpret my suggestions which in many cases, in fact most cases, are but a polite way of giving orders." Washington made it clear that he did not want Tuskegee faculty or staff thinking they "must either object to or debate every order given by the Principal," adding, "I have reasons for every order I give and suggestions that I make in reference to any department."[18]

The more trouble Carver encountered on the campus of Tuskegee, the more he seemed to seek validation of his worth and work from outsiders, especially whites. One of his strongest supporters during those early, troubled days at Tuskegee was James A. Wilson, the Iowa State College professor who had provided him a place to stay when he first arrived in Ames and who had worked with him to welcome new students to the campus during his undergraduate days.

Wilson wrote regularly to Carver, praised his work, offered him advice, and predicted that the efforts of Carver, Booker T. Washington, and others like them would cause "the color line" to "vanish and fade away so thoroughly that people will wonder what was the matter with folks of the 19th century, who established color lines rather than lines of merit, worth, and intelligence."[19]

While Carver was enduring Washington's criticisms, he was becoming increasingly well known away from Tuskegee. A captivating speaker and a creative showman, Carver demonstrated the results of his research at county fairs, at farmers' conferences, and in speeches at schools and churches throughout the region. In February 1898, he published the first of many Experiment Station bulletins, all of them aimed at helping poor southern farmers, especially African Americans, to improve their agricultural practices and their quality of life.

The first three of Carver's bulletins, "Feeding Acorns" (February 1898), "Experiments with Sweet Potatoes" (May 1898), and "Fertilizer Experiments on Cotton" (November 1899), were aimed at suggesting inexpensive ways in which farmers could dramatically increase their agricultural productivity without increasing their outlay of cash for expensive fertilizers. These were ideas that Carver had worked on at Iowa State with James A. Wilson and others.

In April 1900, after receiving Carver's "Bulletin 3, on Fertilizer Experiments on Cotton," Wilson wrote to Carver, pronouncing the bulletin to be "Excellent," and told him, "The more of this kind of plain experimenting you do, the better," adding, "it comes squarely up to the work of the common people all about you."[20]

One of Carver's great gifts, clearly manifested in the publication of his Experiment Station bulletins, was his ability to speak clearly and directly in the language and to the needs of the common people, especially African American farmers. On June 12, 1901, Wilson wrote to Carver, telling him, "The kind of work you are doing is coming into demand everywhere." Wilson informed Carver that he had just been contacted by the president of "North Carolina College of Agriculture," who was in search of a professor of agriculture and was willing to pay $2,500 a year. Wilson told Carver this story because he wanted Carver to know "that is what you are worth to Tuskegee in the future . . . you are a $2,500 man just now." Wilson did understand, however, that the color line continued to matter as the 19th century rolled into the 20th, and he acknowledged that Carver could "probably not get this $2,500" because God "has tinted your skin." Still, Wilson thought Carver should know what he was worth, and Wilson pledged, "when you become a $3,000 man I will tell you so."[21]

Wilson's comment about the color line notwithstanding, Carver did not need to be reminded of persistent problems associated with race in the South. The evidence was all around him. In 1902, he wrote of a harrowing experience he had had in the small town of Ramer, only a short distance from Tuskegee.

A white photographer, Miss Frances B. Johnston, was in Ramer, working on a story about black southern schools. She was picked up at the local train station by a black male teacher, Nelson E. Henry, who drove her in a buggy to his house.

A mob of whites, bothered by the notion of a white woman being accompanied by a black man, threatened to lynch Henry, who was forced to flee the mob and escape the town in the dead of night. Ms. Johnston sought safety in the house where Carver was staying. Carver tried to help her escape from the town unharmed. He also tried to calm and quiet the mob, an effort that not only failed but also placed his own life in jeopardy. As it was, he told Washington, "I had to walk nearly all night Tuesday night to keep out of [the mob's] reach."

No doubt this incident reminded Carver of the lynching he had witnessed some 20 years earlier in Fort Scott, Kansas. The Ramer mob "broke up" the black school. Carver told Washington, "I have never seen people so enraged," adding, "[They] seem to be intensely bitter against any one who comes from Tuskegee."[22]

Meanwhile, Carver continued to find cause for unhappiness at Tuskegee. In November 1901, he complained to Washington, "In fact, the entire agricultural work, in the matter of instructors and instruction, has been exceedingly uncertain, and I think the students feel it." He continued: "At one time we have a class room, at another, none. Sometimes the teacher is present, other times absent; so that the whole work is not up to the standard."[23]

In September 1902, the year of the Ramer incident, six years after arriving at Tuskegee, he wrote a letter to Booker T. Washington that further revealed his frustration and his attitude toward his coworkers. Ostensibly, Carver was trying to get Washington to speak to other teachers and staff and to encourage them to show more interdepartmental cooperation, reiterating in a subtle way his complaint that he was not receiving the assistance from his colleagues that he thought he should.

Having made that point, however, Carver proceeded with a laundry list of behaviors among his Tuskegee coworkers that he thought Washington should try to change. He did not like "the use of slang by the teachers, and especially in the presence of students." He complained about the informality with which teachers addressed each other, using first names to exchange greetings. He told Washington he thought the teaching standards were too low and that faculty members did not take sufficient personal interest in their students, all complaints that no doubt angered his colleagues.[24]

Meanwhile, Carver maintained a schedule that was all-consuming. In January 1904, he wrote again to Washington asking for assistance. In doing so, he outlined his work day: "Today my classes run thus: 8:00 to 9:00, agri. chemistry; 9:20 to 10:00, the foundation and harmony of color to the painter; 10:00 to 12:00, class of farmers, and one period in the afternoon." But that was only the beginning. Additionally, he monitored "seven industrial classes scattered here and there over the grounds"; tested seeds and soil on different plots; examined fertilizers; supervised the poultry yard; and inspected "104 cows that have been inoculated."[25]

Carver's work at Tuskegee had become the focal point of his life. He lived in a dormitory room. He took his meals in the faculty dining room. He seems to have had few close friends at Tuskegee, especially during the first decade and more of his time there. Mostly, he worked, rising before dawn each morning to take a walk in the woods.

Despite all of Carver's hard work at and on behalf of Tuskegee, Booker T. Washington was less than satisfied with him. In 1902, Washington hired George Bridgeforth to assist Carver in the Agricultural Department. One suspects that Washington hoped that the organized and compliant Bridgeforth would serve as an effective antidote to the unorganized and often contrarian Carver. Instead, the younger and less well educated Bridgeforth's presence and preachy criticisms of Carver and the way in which the Agricultural Department was being run exacerbated the tension between Carver and Washington, as well as Carver's feeling of being unappreciated and unvalued.[26]

The main battleground between Bridgeforth and Carver became the handling of the Institute's poultry operation. Bridgeforth condemned Carver's handling of the poultry. His criticism led to an investigation by an ad hoc committee that sided with Bridgeforth and even hinted that Carver had falsified reports to Washington to cover up his own incompetence.

The prideful Carver was incensed. He wrote to tell Washington that "to be branded as a liar and party to such hellish deception . . . is more than I can bear." He offered his resignation, "if your committee feel that I have willfully lied or [am] party to such lies."[27]

Washington did not want Carver to resign. Despite his frustration with the scientist, he knew that Carver was an exemplary teacher and that his work was attracting much-needed attention to Tuskegee. But he did want Carver to be more effective and efficient.

One outgrowth of this battle over the poultry operation was that Bridgeforth tried to persuade Washington to transfer some of Carver's duties to himself. Washington appointed yet another committee to investigate the feasibility and wisdom of that suggestion.

In November 1904, Washington sent Carver a copy of the second committee's report and recommendations. The committee urged Washington to transfer management of the Institute's farm and agricultural production to Bridgeforth, who would assume the title "director of agricultural industries." This would leave Carver in charge of the Experiment Station and of agricultural instruction.

Despite the logic of such a move and the fact that he continually complained of being overworked, Carver responded to this proposal with anger and defiance. In a November 8, 1904, letter to Washington, he told the principal he could "not see my way clear" to accept the recommended changes. He acknowledged embarrassment and a deep concern about what others might think of him, noting that the attendant title change "is too far downward," adding, "A few at Tuskegee will understand it but the public never."[28]

In light of his inability to accept the committee's recommendation and his embarrassment, Carver tendered his resignation yet again, telling Washington he would leave the school "just as soon as I can get the herbarium and cabinets labled [sic] and in place where they will be of the highest service to the school."

Less than a week later, with Washington having taken no action on the committee's recommendations or Carver's response to them, Carver penned a lengthy and somewhat more conciliatory letter to his boss. The new letter was a rambling piece of correspondence that combined a partial acceptance of some of the committee's recommendations with a lengthy explanation of how a lack of support from his coworkers and inadequate resources had led to all of the problems in the first place. He also implied that he would recant his resignation *if* Washington was willing to make some concessions to him, including allowing him to remain in charge of the poultry yard and granting him access to a stenographer for help with the voluminous correspondence he maintained. For good measure, he made a slightly veiled threat that he might still leave Tuskegee if his demands were not met, telling Washington that he had an "unsolicited letter . . . on my desk . . . offering $200 more per year besides other tempting advantages."[29]

Washington did make some concessions to Carver, including allowing him to maintain the title he feared losing and also continuing him on as manager of the much-contested poultry yard. In reducing Carver's responsibilities on campus, Washington expected Carver to do more in the way of outreach work, especially in the production of experiment bulletins. In 1909, Washington complained to Carver that he was not producing bulletins quickly enough: "I cannot feel that your department is doing justice to the matter of getting out the Bulletins." He told Carver that he would provide him some clerical help, thus partially freeing Carver from the burden of not only doing research for the Bulletin but also typing it, although he warned Carver not to "make a mistake of becoming too dependent upon this kind of help."[30]

Despite Washington's concessions, or perhaps at least in part because of them, the principal continued to find fault with what he regarded as Carver's ineffectual management. Four years after the battle between Bridgeforth and Carver began, another conflict emerged, with the poultry yard once again serving as the battleground.

This time the split that Carver had fought off four years earlier was effected: Bridgeforth took over the newly created Department of Agricultural Industries, and Carver was left to manage agricultural instruction and the Experiment Station.[31]

Still, the bickering between Bridgeforth and Carver continued, with Washington left trying to figure out a way he could make the temperamental scientist happy without sacrificing the efficiency and productivity he craved. Over time, a familiar pattern emerged. The exasperated principal would issue an ultimatum to Carver, who, in return, would either ignore the ultimatum or threaten to resign. On occasion, Carver actually sought employment elsewhere. In July 1912, for example, he wrote to James Wilson, telling him, "I think I shall not be here much longer. Please keep me in mind and if you see anything good put me in touch with it." Carver added a statement of justification: "The school has not kept its promise with me and I do not think will, so I am just writing to see what is to be done. I think I have parleyed [sic] with them about long enough."[32] Unfortunately for Carver, no satisfying circumstances presented themselves, and he and Washington plodded on to annoy each other another day.

Such was the stalemate that existed between the two strong-willed men when Washington fell ill in New York City in November 1915 at the age of 59. Aware that he was dying, Washington traveled back to Alabama so that he could end his days at Tuskegee. The end came on November 14, 1915.

Despite the open warfare that had existed between the two men for nearly two decades, Carver was inconsolable at the news of Washington's death. Perhaps he felt guilty at being such a thorn in Washington's side for so many years. Perhaps he regretted not having told Washington how much he admired his accomplishments while he was alive. Perhaps he feared for the future of Tuskegee without Washington at its helm. Three months after Washington's death, Carver wrote to a friend, telling him simply, "I am sure Mr. Washington never knew how much I loved him, and the cause for which he gave his life."[33]

Ironically, Washington's death brought opportunity for Carver in the form of a president, Robert Russa Moton, who admired Carver and his work and gave him something that Washington had always denied him: greater freedom from classroom teaching so that he could focus his time and skills on applied research, aimed at improving the lives of poor southern farmers.

Moton was well aware of his eccentric professor's emerging regional popularity, thanks in no small part to the tribute paid him by Booker T. Washington in his 1911 memoir, titled My Larger Education. In this widely read book, Washington, the man who had done almost daily battle with Carver, praised him as "One of the most gifted men of the Negro race whom I ever happened to meet." He also called Carver "quite the most modest man I have ever met." Subsequently, the Christian Science Monitor published an article by the principal titled "Work of Gifted Negro Teacher is Praised by Dr. Washington."[34]

In giving Carver more time to engage in research and to do public speaking, President Moton hoped that his reputation and, by extension, the reputation of Tuskegee Institute would be enhanced. He could not have imagined then just how successful this strategy would become.

NOTES

1. Linda O. McMurry, *George Washington Carver: Scientist and Symbol* (New York: Oxford University Press, 1981), 51.

2. Interview with Elva Howell. In 1989, Gary R. Kremer interviewed a number of George Washington Carver's former coworkers, students, and friends. The raw footage of these interviews (hereafter referred to as "Kremer Interviews") is housed at the George Washington Carver National Monument in Diamond, Missouri.

3. Louis R. Harlan, ed., *The Booker T. Washington Papers*, vol. 1: *The Autobiographical Writings* (Urbana: University of Illinois Press, 1972), 112.

4. Mark D. Hersey, "'My Work Is That of Conservation': The Environmental Vision of George Washington Carver," Ph.D. diss., University of Kansas, 2006, 202.

5. Quoted in Gary R. Kremer, ed., *George Washington Carver: In His Own Words* (Columbia: University of Missouri Press, 1987), 64–65.

6. George Washington Carver to Mrs. L. H. Pammell, March 30, 1897, Roll 1, frames 0778–0779, George Washington Carver Papers, microfilm edition, compiled and filmed by the National Historical Publication and Records Commission, 1975, Inman E. Page Library, Lincoln University, Jefferson City, MO. Hereafter referred to as "GWC Papers." The original GWC papers are housed at the Tuskegee Institute Archives in Alabama.

7. Population figures are derived from federal census returns, available through Ancestry.com.

8. Hersey, "'My Work Is That of Conservation,'" 199.

9. Kremer, *George Washington Carver*, 8.

10. George Washington Carver to Booker T. Washington, May 19, 1901, GWC Papers, Roll 2, frame 0121.

11. Kremer, *George Washington Carver*, 65–68.

12. Ibid., 65.

13. Ibid., 67.

14. Harlan, *The Booker T. Washington Papers*, vol. 4, 435, 488.

15. Booker T. Washington to George Washington Carver, March 1912, GWC Papers, Roll 5, frame 0071.

16. Quoted in Hersey, "'My Work Is That of Conservation,'" 217.

17. Booker T. Washington to George Washington Carver, April 13, 1912, GWC Papers, Roll 5, frame 0082.

18. Booker T. Washington to George Washington Carver, June (illegible), 1912, GWC Papers, Roll 5, frame 0123.

19. James A. Wilson to George Washington Carver, June 7, 1897, James A. Wilson Papers, Record Series 9/1/11, Box 1, File 18, Letterpress Book 1. Iowa State University Archives, Special Collections Department, Parks Library, Iowa State University, Ames, Iowa. Hereafter referred to as "James A. Wilson Papers."

20. James A. Wilson to George Washington Carver, April 7, 1900, Box 3, File 1, Letterpress Book 7, James A. Wilson Papers.

21. James A. Wilson to Carver, June 12, 1901, Box 3, File 3, Letterpress Book 9, James A. Wilson Papers.

22. Kremer, *George Washington Carver*, 149–51.

23. George Washington Carver to Booker T. Washington, November 3, 1901, GWC Papers, Roll 2, frame 0054.

24. Quoted in Kremer, *George Washington Carver*, 69.

25. Quoted in McMurry, *George Washington Carver*, 57.

26. Ibid., 58–63.

27. Quoted in Kremer, *George Washington Carver*, 70.

28. Ibid., 71–72.

29. Ibid., 72–75.

30. Quoted in McMurry, *George Washington Carver*, 79.

31. Ibid., 65.

32. George Washington Carver to James Wilson, July 2, 1912, GWC Papers, Roll 5, frame 0131.

33. Quoted in Kremer, *George Washington Carver*, 78.

34. Washington devoted nine pages to Carver in a chapter titled "What I Have Learned from Black Men." Booker T. Washington, *My Larger Education; Being Chapters from My Experience* (Garden City, NY: Doubleday, Page, 1911), 223–31; Booker T. Washington, "Work of Gifted Negro Teacher Is Praised by Dr. Washington," *Christian Science Monitor*, December 21, 1912, 11.

Chapter 5

CARVER THE TEACHER

You are a great teacher . . . a great inspirer of young men.

—*Booker T. Washington, letter to George Washington Carver*

George Washington Carver may have been inept as a manager. He may have been arrogant and demanding. He may have been a thorn in the side of efficiency-minded Tuskegee administrators. But no one could deny that he was a skilled teacher. Even Booker T. Washington, whose patience Carver repeatedly tried, recognized this fact. In 1911, at the height of one of his many conflicts with the professor and after chastising him for multiple failings, Washington nonetheless praised Carver's skill as an instructor: "You are a great teacher, a great lecturer, a great inspirer of young men and old men; that is your forte."[1]

Likewise, Washington's successor, Robert Russa Moton, recognized Carver's brilliance as a teacher. In June 1916, Carver wrote to Moton that a variety of personal concerns, including his despondency over Washington's death, made it impossible for him to teach his "usual classes in botany for the coming year." Moton received Carver's letter while on a trip away from Tuskegee but quickly wrote to him, asking the professor to delay any final decision until Moton had a chance to talk with him. "I need not tell you," Moton stated, "that it will be impossible to get anybody to teach this subject as you have done, and I do not like to think of the students losing the inspiration and help that would come by your teaching."[2]

Carver needed all the skill he could muster when he first stepped into a Tuskegee classroom in the fall of 1896. The challenges were legion. Like other black teachers in racially segregated southern schools, Carver had to make do with inadequate resources and equipment. He had no real laboratory in which he could conduct research and from which he could teach. He had one microscope, a farewell gift from the faculty and his fellow students at Iowa State. Indeed, soon after arriving at Tuskegee, Carver wrote a "thank you" card that was published in the Iowa Agricultural College student paper. He told his former colleagues, "This evening as I sit at my writing desk in the sunny south-land, I wish I could make you feel how thankful I am for the beautiful and useful presents you so kindly gave me." Perhaps he should have stopped there, but the missionary complex that seemed to influence his adjustment to his new circumstances would not allow him to do so, and he went on to write, "You who have no such problems to face as I have here can scarcely appreciate their usefulness to me."[3] Recalling the inadequacy of equipment available to him upon his arrival at Tuskegee some years later, Carver remembered how he addressed the problem: "I went to the trash pile of Tuskegee Institute, and started my laboratory with bottles, old fruit jars and any other thing I found I could use."[4] His office remained unheated as late as the fall of 1900, although he stoically wrote Washington, "I think I can get along this winter."[5] Indeed, more than a decade and a half after his arrival at Tuskegee, Carver wrote caustically to the principal, complaining that the equipment available to him was still inadequate: "I do not think it fair for us to deceive ourselves and think we have a workable laboratory when we have not."[6]

The students that Carver had studied with at Simpson College and Iowa State came primarily from families whose parents were high school graduates. By contrast, the students that Carver taught at Tuskegee were hardly prepared for rigorous academic work. They were, for the most part, the children and grandchildren of slaves who had been denied access to education by Alabama law. Their parents were barely literate at best. There was no tradition of learning and study among them, no knowledge of what it might take to succeed academically, no appreciation of the benefits of learning.

As an instructor of agriculture in a rural, segregated southern school, Carver faced an especially daunting challenge: these African American tillers of the soil were sure they knew how to farm. They knew because their parents had taught them. They also knew the futility of trying to make a living off the land. Their parents had taught them that, as well. Many young men came to Tuskegee because they wanted to escape farming. They preferred, instead, to learn a skill, such as carpentry or shoemaking, even though they likely faced a future as a tiller of someone else's soil.

Carver possessed the skills that always are the hallmark of good teachers, or, as the *Savannah Morning News* commented in 1903: "Carver has the two essentials of a good teacher;—a thorough knowledge of his work, and a knowledge of how to teach it." The paper added,

Initially Carver's laboratory at Tuskegee was inadequately equipped. In addition to his laboratory research, his duties included teaching, field research, and management of the school's farm, which was essential to its solvency. (Courtesy of the Tuskegee University Archives)

"There are only five or six such men in the country."[7] He cared deeply about his students. He involved himself in every aspect of their lives, a task made easier by the fact that he lived among them in a dormitory known as Rockefeller Hall and often took his meals with them, instead of eating with the rest of the faculty. Students corresponding with him in the years after they left Tuskegee often made reference to dining with Carver. One former student, for example, wrote to tell Carver, "I often think of the good laughs we used to have at the table."[8] Another, referring to Carver as "My own Bro. 'Sunshine,'" told the professor, "don't let any of those folks at the table tread on you."[9]

Carver was available and approachable. Students sought him out to discuss their problems, academic, personal, and financial. It was not unheard of for the professor to receive requests for loans from current and former students, such as this one: "Prof. I am not a beggar nor would I do an unmanly act with anybody for anything. I need this $100 and I am asking you for it."[10] At least sometimes, he complied with such requests. Carver biographer Ethel Edwards wrote that, in 1928 alone, Carver gave individual Tuskegee Institute students a total of $179.40.[11]

At times, Carver took up the causes of students who, like himself, found themselves in conflict with the rigid Tuskegee administration. Such was the case in late 1912, when school treasurer Warren Logan tried to force student Monsees Cohen to pay an overdue bill for $72. Cohen had been the victim of either an accident or illness the previous summer. As a consequence, he had been hospitalized numerous times during the fall semester and was confined when Carver wrote to Booker T. Washington on his behalf on December 13, 1912. Assuring the principal that Monsees "has only $50.00 at his disposal," Carver sought understanding and debt relief for his student. It must have been extremely gratifying for the student to have the professor as his advocate.[12]

While Carver often seemed whiney and cranky and aloof to Tuskegee administrators, faculty, and staff, students saw him as a fun-loving prankster who joked and played with them. One of Carver's favorite games was the somewhat unusual practice of administering mock whippings to his students, something that is well documented through a large correspondence with his current and former students through the years. One student, away from Tuskegee for the summer in 1917, wrote to Carver, telling him, "Of course you miss beating me and I miss my beatings but perhaps I will be able to get them before long."[13] A former student, writing to Carver from faraway Kansas, teased his old mentor by telling him he was no longer within his reach: "Well, I don't think I will ever need any more beating up. . . . I can't be bothered about having my back pained that way Ha! Ha! . . . I don't have to dodge when I say that because you can't reach me now." The former student, who had become a teacher in Manhattan, Kansas, signed himself, "Your Faithful Pupil."[14] Similarly, another former student wrote a playful letter to Carver, telling the professor, "I suppose you really and truly feel like giving me a good spanking," adding a warning: "well, your 'use-to be boy ["boy" underlined twice]' is now at home with his wife and he feels that it would take a pretty good man to handle him."[15] Likewise, Ambrose Caliver, a Tuskegee graduate who taught manual training at Fisk University, wrote to Carver in 1917, telling him, "I know that you have laid me to the dogs and that you would like to lay the dogs (dogwood) to me," although he too warned his former teacher, "but you know I am married now and you cannot whip a married man. SEE!!!"

The esteem with which Caliver viewed Carver is evidenced by the former's comment, "Mrs. Caliver said she is very anxious to meet you and that she believes she could become your little girl just as her MOST WONDERFUL and precious husband has become your BIG boy or rather MAN [underlined]."[16] Yet another former student remembered decades after the fact that Carver would sometimes chase students up and down the stairs and through the hallways of Millbank Hall, where his office was located, with a rolled-up newspaper, feigning anger that his quiet time had been disrupted by rowdy, noisy young men and shouting warnings, such as, "Don't you do that again."[17]

Carver's ability to tease and be teased by students was legendary. One of the most famous stories associated with Carver's teaching days emerged from an effort by students to stump the professor by creating an allegedly new breed of insect by assembling body parts from a variety of cadavers into a "new" species and asking the professor if he could identify it. He did so immediately, pronouncing it to be a "humbug." The students who engaged in this lighthearted farce must have felt safe in their game, knowing that their teacher would enjoy their effort to fool him as much as they did.[18]

In the classroom or on the lecture circuit, Carver was anything but traditional. He was a showman and a storyteller who eschewed long, formal abstract lectures in favor of concrete demonstrations. One witness to a presentation commented, "The most striking thing about him is his eyes, which are deep black but which seem to have two gleaming coals of living fire behind them."[19] In 1928, Elva Howell, then a college student in her early twenties at Virginia State College in Petersburg, had a close encounter with Carver's unconventional methods. In a 1989 interview, Howell remembered going to chapel one day for a lecture that required all students' attendance. "This tall, spare man was seated up on the rostrum," she recalled. "We did not know who he was. . . . When [he] came to the lectern . . . he had a sweet potato in his hand. He put the sweet potato up on the lectern and he said, in his high voice, 'I said, sweet potato, sweet potato, what are you?'" Howell remembered, "The reaction of the student body was a great deal of laughter, at whoever heard of asking a sweet potato, 'what are you?'" Only later did she discover that "we were in the presence of one of the world's great scientists."[20] Alternatively, Carver might display a plant or an insect collected on an early morning walk and ask students to help him to identify it or to discern the circumstances under which it would grow best or the soil conditions that would nurture it most.

Above all, Carver taught inquisitiveness and encouraged creative thought; he introduced his students to the world of the mind. "This old notion," he once wrote, "of swallowing down other people's ideas and problems just as they have worked them out, without putting our brain and origionality [sic] into it, and making them applicable to our specific [needs] must go. And the sooner we let them go the sooner we will be a free and indipendent [sic] people."[21] He often quoted to his students a poem by Edgar A. Guest titled "Equipment." The poem begins with the line "Figure it out for yourself, my lad," and emphasizes that God has equipped all people with the basic tools they need to succeed.

Carver made his students work to understand the lessons he wanted them to learn. In a late-life interview, former student Edward Pryce remembered Carver's teaching technique in this way: "I'd go in and ask him the name of this plant and he would never tell you a thing. He wouldn't answer your question. He was like Socrates, he would ask another question, and that would lead you into the answer, but you had to work for it." Pryce continued: "I can remember his saying, I can tell you the family, but you'll have to get your . . . botanical key, and look this thing up yourself." Carver would prod Pryce by urging him to look at the underside of the leaves of the plant and to take note of its color. "He was teaching me how to observe," Pryce recalled, forcing him to come to conclusions on his own.[22]

Additionally, Carver demanded accuracy and thoroughness from his students. He was uninterested in allowing students to engage in uninformed discussions during which they might merely exchange ignorances. "Students invariably want to discuss the topic, rather than give you a direct answer," he wrote on one occasion. "This is not permissible, neither what he or she may think, unless their thoughts are based on facts." He added: "There is nothing to be deplored more in the classroom than to hear a number of pupils pretending to recite, and constantly telling you what they think with reference to matters that the intellectual world has recognized as facts decades ago."[23] One former student recalled in a late-life interview an occasion when he began a sentence, addressing Carver with the words, "Dr. Carver, I think. . . ." Carver cut him off with the caustic query "Now who accused you of being able to think?"[24]

Carver wanted to help his students to understand the complex world in which they lived by understanding first and foremost what he regarded as a simple truth: that the natural world is a gift from God to humanity, that the world is understandable, and that it contains all of the resources people need for healthy and productive living. Humanity's job is to figure out how best to make use of those resources, how to take the gifts of God and make them of use to people. That Carver succeeded is evidenced in the letters he received from current and former students, including a poignant note written by J. H. Ward, a 1910 graduate of Tuskegee, who wrote to Carver seven years after he left the classroom. Like many of Carver's other correspondents who addressed him as a parent, Ward called Carver "My dear 'Father.'" He began the letter by writing, "Guess you think your son has been silent a long time." He continued, "But you know how sons are when they leave home with the determination of accomplishing great things. They like to do a few things before letting their parents know about them."

Ward emphasized his "wish to write to you as I would my own father" and explained to Carver what studying under the professor had meant to him in words that sounded much like the professor's own: "My whole soul has been centered upon every movement along agricultural and literary lines in connection with Tuskegee ever since I left; but most, especially, [sic] upon agricultural lines. Indeed, I deem it the only profession and occupation which brings men really in touch with God, in the truest sense."[25]

Carver was at all times a preeminent conservationist, and he wanted his students to understand the need to avoid waste. Elaine Thomas, the daughter of a Tuskegee faculty member, grew up hanging out in Carver's laboratory. Addressed by the professor always as "little girl," Thomas remembered how Carver saved twine from packages delivered to his office. He saved the twine and used it to macrame, telling Thomas, "You and others pitch this sort of thing. I find a second use for everything."[26]

One of Carver's greatest gifts as a teacher was his ability to see the potential for growth in his students and his ability to nurture their nascent curiosities. Even as a graduate student at Iowa State College, Carver had exhibited this special talent in his relationship with Henry A. Wallace, a future vice president of the United States. In later life, Wallace, the son of Iowa State faculty member Henry C. Wallace, recalled how Carver took him, a six-year-old boy, out collecting. As Wallace remembered it, "Because of his friendship with my father, and perhaps his interest in children, George Carver often took me with him on his botany expeditions, and it was he who introduced me to the mysteries of plant fertilization" and "deepen[ed] my appreciation of plants in a way I could never forget."[27]

At Tuskegee, Carver continued to be drawn especially to children and to relish the opportunity to teach them about the beauty and mystery of the natural world. He made gifts for them and painted small landscape scenes on note cards for their birthdays and for Christmas. His interest in children seems to have been particularly strong during the second half of the first decade of the 20th century. This interest corresponded with and was likely nurtured by his roughly three-year courtship of Miss Sarah L. Hunt, the sister-in-law of Tuskegee Institute Treasurer Warren Logan. The relationship ended in 1907, when Miss Hunt took a teaching job in California.

While at Tuskegee, according to Carver biographer Ethel Edwards, Hunt taught the fourth grade at what was known as "Children's House," the elementary school for children of Tuskegee employees. During this time, Carver "developed an extraordinary interest in juvenile agriculture." He visited Ms. Hunt's classroom regularly and helped her students to plan, plant, and harvest gardens.[28] No doubt this activity contributed greatly to his production of a bulletin titled "Nature Study and Gardening for Rural Schools," in 1910.[29]

In this publication, Carver proclaimed his "chief mission" to be to awaken "a greater interest in practical nature lessons in the public schools of our section" and "To bring before our young people in an attractive way a few of the cardinal principles of agriculture." Carver endorsed the idea of "a very large part of the child's education" occurring "outside of the four walls designated as class room." He also urged the schools to begin "nature study" with "the wee tots, the kindergarteners." He urged teachers to think of gardening as a way of teaching "composition, spelling, reading, arithmetic, geography, and history." He followed with elaborate instructions for teachers that included labor contracts between students and teachers and instructions on how to care for tools, prepare soil, select and test seeds, plant, cultivate, harvest and market crops, and much more. In short, the bulletin was designed to introduce to children all the concepts about conservation and agriculture that Carver was elsewhere trying to teach college students and adults. He seemed to understand that children were impressionable and excited about learning, and he hoped to capitalize on those characteristics. "Instinctively," he believed, "they prefer to deal with natural objects and real things."[30]

Carver seems to have sustained his special interest in children throughout much, if not all, of his career at Tuskegee. Yet another example of his relationship with children can be gleaned from a letter written to him in late 1942, only four days before his death. The letter was from a Morgantown, North Carolina, teacher who recalled that, more than 17 years earlier, in August 1925, he, his wife and their three children had visited Carver in his Tuskegee laboratory. Oscar Randolph remembered, "Even though our youngest boy was only 2 ½ years of age at the time, you were so kind, fatherly, and unusually courteous and friendly towards children that he continues to say that he remembers you quite well." Randolph added, "He used to speak of you as 'Uncle Carver.'"[31]

Early in his second decade at Tuskegee, Carver taught an informal Bible study class that eventually attracted a regular group of hundreds of young students, much as his mentor, Professor James Wilson, had done many years before at Iowa State. In 1916, Carver reminisced about the origins of this class: "My Bible class was started 10 years ago by Mr. Beecher Norton, then my office boy. With several other students he met and decided that they wanted to use the few minutes between supper and the chapel hour every Sunday evening in reading the Bible." As Carver remembered it, the group chose him to be its teacher. Initially, he hesitated, but then he consented, after concluding, "here was a fine opportunity to parallel science and religion, and to show that there was no conflict between them."[32]

In a late-life interview more than seven decades after the fact, Harold Webb recalled attending Carver's Sunday school for two years after his arrival at Tuskegee, in 1915. Webb emphasized that Carver "knew the Bible and he was a good Sunday School teacher for me." Carver, he remembered, "recited all the parables to us," adding, "In his class, I learned all about old Zachariah skinnying down that Sycamore tree and . . . about Daniel and the Lion's den . . ., the Hebrew children and the fiery furnace. . . . All of that he made quite clear to us." Webb remembered that Carver would sometimes take an entire study period to explain one parable, and that he did so with great clarity and simplicity. Webb added that Carver was "quite friendly" and that he "talked to the students quite a bit. You could stop him on the street anywhere and talk with him. Very seldom he was too busy to stop and tell you or show you something."[33] Likewise, William Dawson, who ran away from home as a 13-year-old boy so that he could attend Tuskegee, remembered that students arrived on the second floor of Carnegie Hall on the campus for Carver's Sunday school class very early to ensure that they would get one of the much-in-demand seats. The students would ask Carver questions about the Bible, and Carver would respond to their questions. "That was," Dawson recalled, "a wonderful experience."[34]

Yet another former Bible class student, J. D. Reed, wrote to Carver some years after he left Tuskegee to tell the professor, "Perhaps you would be interested to know how I am being help[ed] by our Bible class." Reed credited a testimonial about the Bible class that he delivered at a church with helping him to get a good job in a leather factory. He concluded that he was proud to have been a member of Carver's Bible class and assured Carver, "I feel very much indebted to you for it."[35] Likewise, Oscar Parks of Council Bluffs, Iowa, wrote to tell Carver, "I take pleasure in writing you a few lines to let you know I have not forgotten you and your wonderful Bible class." Parks added, "I have often wished for those few minutes spent with you and the boys and can appreciate the value of them more than ever before."[36] Similarly, former student Alphonso Sellers told Carver, "I miss you so much here—especially the 'Bible Class' which I was so very fond off [sic]." Sellers went on to tell Carver, "It seems to me like I can hear you every Sunday evening." He urged Carver to tell his students "to take advantage of that opportunity because it is not found anywhere else except Tuskegee." Sellers summed up his feelings by telling Carver, "your Bible Class added more to my education than anything else in school. I am sorry I cannot be there anymore under your instruction."[37]

Carver's involvement with his students did not end when they graduated or left the school. Many students stayed in touch with him through correspondence, and students often came back to Tuskegee to visit him. Some sought his advice and encouragement from afar, much as they had when they still lived at Tuskegee. Some even tried to emulate Carver and Washington after leaving school by trying to set up "little Tuskegees" elsewhere in the country.

One young man in this latter group was Nathaniel C. Bruce. Born in 1868 in Virginia, Bruce studied under Carver before traveling to Missouri to establish, in 1907, a school that he informally referred to as "the Tuskegee of the Midwest." In a letter to Carver some years later, Bruce expressed a sentiment that no doubt caused Carver to harken back to his early days in Alabama: "Under our Missouri conditions, what I am working hardest on is food—two sorts of food, in fact—material food and mental food." Bruce added, "I find that the Missouri Negro is far behind in the matter of general intelligence; so he needs mental food as well as material food."[38]

Similarly, in 1914, H. B. Bennett, a former student of Carver's, wrote to the professor to report on his work in Shallo, Mississippi. Addressing

Carver as "Dear Father," Bennet thanked Carver for a recent letter, evidencing the existence of a two-way correspondence, and then tellingly went on to inform his mentor, "If you had any idea what you have done in this community through me, I am sure you could die happy." Bennet had been conducting a school in Mississippi for the previous five years. He felt he had achieved great success, all of which he attributed to lessons taught him by Carver. He told Carver, "it is you who laid the foundation for my life's journey," adding, "I would have failed time and again had it not been for your good instruction." Bennett concluded his praise of Carver by assuring him, "this is not my victory; it is yours." Lofty praise, indeed, for a former teacher.[39]

There is a high level of intimacy and trust in the letters that Carver's former students wrote to him, characteristics that testify to the strength of the bond between them and him. One young woman, a former Tuskegee Institute student, wrote to thank Carver for a letter and a package of undisclosed contents. She told Carver about her efforts to conserve resources of all kinds: "From the savings of grease from my kitchen I have made one hundred and sixty pounds of soap which is beautiful." The student went on to talk about her vegetable and flower gardens but then abruptly began to share with Carver her anxieties about "my boy," her boyfriend, Emory. After two paragraphs in which she expressed multiple worries about the relationship, she concluded somewhat philosophically, "I am going to do all that I can for him and if I loose [sic] him I will know that I did my part by him."[40]

Clearly, Carver had a tremendous impact upon the lives of his students, and he continued to influence and shape them long after they left his direct tutelage. Often students wrote to him asking for letters of reference as they sought admission to graduate schools or jobs. Carver eagerly wrote letters of endorsement, even if, on occasion, the endorsements were less than ringing. Such was the case, for example, in 1930, when a student, George E. Majette, of Lawrenceville, Virginia, asked Carver to write a letter on his behalf to the Julius Rosenwald Fund in Chicago. Carver wrote the letter of support, indicating, "I taught him as a student and have been once to see his farm, etc.," but then added, "Here he was a very good average scholar, not one of those very brilliant kind, but a plodder and did good work."[41] No doubt this letter left Majette less than appreciative of Carver's total honesty.

Carver maintained a correspondence with former students throughout his life. In late 1942, years after he had retired from the classroom and only weeks before his death, he received a letter from a student that summed up what many who had encountered him through his many years at Tuskegee must have felt. "I have been thinking about you all the week," the former student began. "The longer I live and the more I see, time brings a brighter picture of the things that you taught me. Surely your experiences are unparalleled [sic] to none. . . . I am reminded of the days you would call us in and talk about the many rich things of life." He signed the letter, "Your son, Joseph."[42]

Ironically, this unmarried, fatherless teacher seemingly wanted to be a dad to all of his students. And they, or at least many of them, welcomed the opportunity to be his surrogate children, his "boys" and "girls," sharing their life stories and their secrets with him and, like children of all ages, trying to impress the "parent" they admired so much. For a man so unhappy with Tuskegee administrators and colleagues, Carver found his relationship with students to be an emotional bond that helped to sustain him.

NOTES

1. Quoted in Linda O. McMurry, *George Washington Carver: Scientist and Symbol* (New York: Oxford University Press, 1981), 68.

2. Robert Russa Moton to George Washington Carver, June 10, 1916, Roll 5, frame 0660, George Washington Carver Papers, microfilm edition, compiled and filmed by the National Historical Publication and Records Commission, 1975, Inman E. Page Library, Lincoln University, Jefferson City, MO. Hereafter referred to as "GWC Papers." The original GWC papers are housed at the Tuskegee Institute Archives in Alabama.

3. Quoted in Mark D. Hersey, "'My Work Is That of Conservation': The Environmental Vision of George Washington Carver," Ph.D. diss., University of Kansas, 2006, 103.

4. Quoted in McMurry, *George Washington Carver*, 130.

5. George Washington Carver to Booker T. Washington, November 23, 1900, GWC Papers, Roll 2, frame 0060.

6. George Washington Carver to Booker T. Washington, December 20, 1912, GWC Papers, Roll 5, frame 0238.

7. Quoted in a letter from George Washington Carver to Booker T. Washington, March 3, 1903, GWC Papers, Roll 2, frame 0559.

8. M.L. Carrington to George Washington Carver, August 15, 1917, GWC Papers, Roll 5, 0798.

9. Dan Rudolph to George Washington Carver, undated, probably 1917, GWC Papers, Roll 5, frames 0967–0968.

10. J.A. Taylor to George Washington Carver, December 10, 1917, GWC Papers, Roll 5, frame 0937.

11. Ethel Edwards, *Carver of Tuskegee* (Cincinnati, OH: Psyche Press, 1971), 165.

12. George Washington Carver to Booker T. Washington, December 13, 1912, GWC Papers, Roll 5, frame 0222.

13. H.H. Boyes to George Washington Carver, July 9, 1917, GWC Papers, GWC Papers, Roll 5, frame 0735.

14. J.L. Campbell to George Washington Carver, May 28, 1917, GWC Papers, Roll 5, frames 0702–0703.

15. "Your 'Tod of the Swamps'" to George Washington Carver, August 8, 1917, GWC Papers, Roll 5, frames 0785–0786.

16. Ambrose Caliver to George Washington Carver, December 1, 1917, GWC Papers, Roll 5, frame 0925.

17. Edward Pryce interview, Kremer Interviews.

18. McMurry, *George Washington Carver*, 99.

19. Quoted in ibid., 150.

20. Elva Howell interview, Kremer Interviews.

21. Quoted in McMurry, *George Washington Carver*, 104.

22. Edward Pryce interview, Kremer Interviews.

23. Quoted in Hersey, "'My Work Is That of Conservation,'" 253.

24. William Dawson interview, Kremer Interviews.

25. J.H. Ward to George Washington Carver, October 10, 1917, GWC Papers, Roll 5, frames 0870–0872.

26. Elaine Thomas interview, Kremer Interviews.

27. Quoted in Rackham Holt, *George Washington Carver: An American Biography*, rev. ed. (Garden City, NY: Doubleday, 1943), 101.

28. Edwards, *Carver of Tuskegee*, 72–73.

29. George Washington Carver, "Nature Study and Gardening for Rural Schools," Tuskegee Experiment Station, Bulletin No. 18 (June 1910).

30. Ibid., 3–4.

31. E. Oscar Randolph to George Washington Carver, December 31, 1942, GWC Papers, Roll 43, frame 1227.

32. George Washington Carver to "My Dear Mr. Griffin," July 2, 1916, GWC Papers, Roll 5, frame 0665.

33. Harold Webb interview, Kremer Interviews.

34. William Dawson interview, Kremer Interviews.

35. J. D. Reed to George Washington Carver, July 15, 1917, GWC Papers, Roll 5, frames 0743–0745.

36. Oscar Parks to George Washington Carver, July 16, 1917, GWC Papers, Roll 5, frames 0750–0751.

37. Alphonso Sellers to George Washington Carver, September 24, 1917, GWC Papers, Roll 5, frames 0849–0850.

38. N. C. Bruce to George Washington Carver, May 28, 1917, GWC Papers, Roll 5, frame 0701.

39. H. B. Bennett to George Washington Carver, February 27, 1914, GWC Papers, Roll 5, frames 0365–0367.

40. A. O. Barns to George Washington Carver, July 16, 1917, GWC Papers, Roll 5, frame 0746.

41. George Washington Carver to George R. Arthur, March 24, 1930, GWC Papers, Roll 12, frame 0048.

42. George W. Haynes to George Washington Carver, October 24, 1942, GWC Papers, Roll 43, frames 329–330.

Chapter 6

THE EFFORT TO TRANSFORM
SOUTHERN AGRICULTURE

My idea is to help the "man farthest down."

—*George Washington Carver, letter to "My dear Mr. Flood"*

Booker T. Washington did not bring George Washington Carver to Alabama merely to teach the hundreds of students who attended Tuskegee Institute each year. Rather, Washington expected Carver also to instruct the larger black community of Macon County, the state of Alabama, even the entire African American South.

The vast majority of black Southerners were mired in a culture of economic dependency on whites in the 1890s. Most blacks made their living as sharecroppers and tenant farmers, working for whites who continued to try to make a living off of growing the South's still-dominant cash crop, King Cotton. Indeed, according to historian R. Douglas Hurt, even as late as 1900, four years after Carver's arrival at Tuskegee, "tenancy in the South bound most of the 707,364 black farmers to the land. . . . [A]bout 75 percent of all black farmers were tenants, usually sharecroppers. With more than half a million black farmers captive to the trinity of cotton, tenancy, and poverty, they were a desperate people with little hope."[1]

Alabama whites liked it that way, for, just as African Americans depended on white landowners to provide them with jobs as agricultural laborers, whites understood that the profitability and viability of their farms and plantations depended on the large pool of unskilled and poorly educated African American farm laborers who dominated the agricultural work force in the Black Belt. Many, no doubt, agreed with the popular white newspaper columnist Charles Henry Smith, whose column appeared under the pen name "Bill Arp" in hundreds of southern weekly newspapers during the late 19th century. According to Arp, "The masses of the negro race are never so happy as when in the cornfield or the cotton patch and being dependent upon the white man for protection and advice."[2]

Indeed, at precisely the time that Booker T. Washington and George Washington Carver were trying to help blacks become more economically independent of whites, at least some white landowners in Alabama were trying to re-enslave black males by devising a plethora of schemes aimed at forcing them to work for whites for little or no pay, in virtual slave circumstances.[3] Among the most egregious examples of whites "enslaving" blacks through peonage and vagrancy laws during the last quarter of the 19th century was the case of Alabama plantation owner John Pace, who lived less than 50 miles from Tuskegee. For decades into the early 20th century, according to author Douglas A. Blackmon, Pace "purchased" African Americans "convicted" of petty crimes from county officials and forced them to work on his farm under the supervision of armed guards and dogs trained to track escapees. The workers were bound and chained at night and beaten mercilessly when they refused to comply with directions.[4]

Booker T. Washington had begun an effort in 1892, four years before Carver's arrival at Tuskegee, to teach blacks how to improve the productivity and profitability of their agricultural activities. In that year, he hosted the first of what would become an annual farmers' conference, through which he tried to teach African American farmers how to improve their agricultural practices. As historian Allen Jones points out, "the guiding theme and philosophy of the farmers' conference was Washington's sermons on agricultural diversification, self-sufficiency, and self-improvement."[5] Washington had no idea how many farmers would show up at the first conference in 1892. To his surprise, more than 400 men and women appeared.

The farmers who attended that first conference came out of recognition that they needed help. They reported to Washington "frankly and simply that four-fifths of them lived on rented land in small one-room cabins and mortgaged their crops for food on which to live." Before the conference ended, the farmers adopted the following resolution:

> The seriousness of our condition lies in that, in the States where the colored people are most numerous, at least 90 percent of them are in the country, they are difficult to reach, and but little is being done for them. Their industrial, educational and moral condition is slowly improving, but among the masses there is still a great amount of poverty and ignorance and much need of moral and religious training.
>
> We urge all to buy land and to cultivate it thoroughly; to raise more food supplies; to build homes with more than one room; to tax themselves to build better school-houses, and to extend the school term to at least six months; to give more attention to the character of our leaders, especially ministers and teachers; to keep out of debt; to avoid lawsuits; to treat our women better; and that conferences similar in aim to this one be held in every community where practicable.[6]

Booker T. Washington, of course, expected George Washington Carver to expand the annual Farmers' Conference and to assist the farmers in achieving their goals. But this was a serious challenge for Carver, who was unfamiliar with the South, its people, its soil, and its climate. Late in his life, he recalled the shock he experienced on his first trip to Alabama, in October 1896: "When my train left the golden wheat fields and the tall green corn of Iowa for the acres of cotton, nothing but cotton, my heart sank a little. . . . The scraggly cotton grew close up to the cabin doors; a few lonesome collards, the only sign of vegetables; stunted cattle, boney mules; fields and hill sides cracked and scarred with gullies and deep ruts . . . not much evidence of scientific farming anywhere. Everything looked hungry: the land, the cotton, the cattle, and the people."[7] Indeed, historian Mark Hersey has pointed out that even a half-century before Carver arrived at Tuskegee, "the county's single greatest agricultural problem was erosion, and cotton cultivation was the single biggest contributor to it."[8]

One of the first things Carver did during his early tenure at Tuskegee was to undertake a series of experiments through which he tried to understand what plants would grow well in the Alabama soil and which ones would help to build up the soil and provide good forage. Understanding that black Macon County farmers did not have money for expensive seeds and fertilizers, he attempted to focus on techniques that would cost farmers little more than their own hard labor and ingenuity.

In 1898, less than two years after his arrival at Tuskegee, Carver published two of the scores of bulletins he would produce over the course of the next four decades, all of them aimed at improving the lives of black southern farmers. The brilliance of these bulletins lay in the simple, straightforward manner in which he communicated his message to a marginally educated audience.

Bulletin No. 1, "Feeding Acorns," introduced farmers to the notion that they could take the lowly and abundant acorn, available without cost to them wherever oak trees grew, and transform it into an inexpensive source of livestock feed.[9] This was a classic Carver innovation: take something that was produced by nature and that was widely regarded as a valueless waste product, and transform it into a valuable and useful commodity. Indeed, the acorn was regarded as so valueless that many of Carver's coworkers scoffed at the notion that it might have utility. As Carver told Washington, "I was even accused to my face (by a teacher in high authority) as going crazy."[10]

Simultaneously, Carver produced a second bulletin in 1898, this one titled "Experiments with Sweet Potatoes." This publication was informed, first of all, by Carver's acute awareness of how damaged the Alabama soil was by the poor land management practices of Alabama farmers, including the depletion of the soil's nutrients by the repeated growth of cotton and the failure to restore the soil's nutrients once they had been drained from it.[11]

Carver had begun his experiments with sweet potatoes in 1897. He chose the sweet potato, he later wrote, because "More bushels of sweet potatoes can be raised per acre than any other farm crop, with less injury to [the] soil."[12] One of his great innovations with regard to sweet potato production came in the way he prepared the soil. Deeply concerned about topsoil erosion and the lack of fertility of Alabama topsoil after so many years of producing cotton and convinced that deep plowing of the soil would bring more nutritious soil elements to the surface, thereby reducing erosion and improving the quality of the plants in the soil, Carver resolved to use something almost unheard of in the Black Belt of Alabama—a two-horse, as opposed to a one-horse, plow! Years later, Carver remembered, "Nobody had a two-horse plow. I asked for one and they thought I had lost every bit of gray matter that I had," something that no doubt contributed to the image of Carver as an eccentric outsider who perhaps did not know what he was talking about.[13]

Carver's desire to produce sweet potatoes was driven, also, by his desire to supplement the poor Southerner's diet. For one thing, the ever-frugal Booker T. Washington had charged Carver with responsibility for improving the diet of Tuskegee faculty and students, while simultaneously reducing the school's costs for foodstuffs. Once, when he was on a trip away from the school, Washington wrote to Carver, telling him, "By the time I reach Tuskegee, I wish you would let me have a list of all the vegetables, berries and fruits growing in Macon County that can be either preserved or canned."[14]

Carver was also concerned about the adverse effects of poor diets that he saw evidenced in the bodies of many of his students from Macon County and other parts of the rural South, many of whom came from families that subsisted on contaminated corn products, primarily grits and cornbread. In 1896, a U.S. Department of Agriculture study described the daily diet of Alabama's African American farmers: "The daily fare is prepared in very simple ways. Corn meal is mixed with water and baked on the flat surface of a hoe or griddle. The salt pork is sliced thin and fried until very brown and much of the grease [f]ried out. Molasses from cane or sorghum is added to the fat, making what is known as 'sap,' which is eaten with the corn bread. . . . This is the bill of fare of most of the cabins on the plantations of the 'black belt,' three times a day during the year."[15]

The first decade of Carver's tenure in Alabama coincided with the era in which pellagra was beginning to be diagnosed among poor Southerners. In 1902, a Georgia physician, Dr. H. F. Harris, presented a paper at a meeting of that state's Medical Association in which he reported on a recently diagnosed case of pellagra he had treated in a poor Georgia farmer. Long known as a debilitating, deadly disease in Europe, pellagra was not documented or acknowledged in the United States until the 20th century.

Four years after Dr. Harris's report, medical authorities in Alabama found themselves dealing with an epidemic of pellagra at the state's Mount Vernon Insane Hospital, a segregated facility for African Americans about 200 miles from Tuskegee. Eighty-eight of the hospital's inmates contracted pellagra, and nearly two-thirds of them died, a shocking development that made the disease a plague-like challenge to a generation of poor Southerners and their caregivers.

Dr. Harris laid the blame for pellagra on the consumption of contaminated corn products, usually grits and cornbread, both staples of the poor Southerner's diet. When Dr. George H. Searcy discovered pellagra among the Mount Vernon Insane Hospital's patients, he sent a cornmeal sample to a laboratory for analysis. Tests concluded that the cornmeal "was made of moldy grain and contained rather large quantities of a variety of bacteria and fungi."[16]

Dr. Harris's conclusion as to the cause of pellagra stood the scrutiny of scientific analysis. But a cure for pellagra, the introduction of variety into the poor Southerner's diet, the ability to avoid contaminated corn, and greater access to high protein foods was not so easily achieved. These became important goals of Carver's as he tried to add diversity to the diets of poor African American farmers as a way of battling this debilitating disease. His most direct and extensive comments on pellagra came in a bulletin titled "Three Delicious Meals Every Day for the Farmer." Drawing upon studies by "Government experts," he argued that "Pellagra is alarmingly on the increase, and that it is due largely to an unbalanced ration; or, in other words, there is not variety enough in the diet; and that this terrible disease may be prevented and many cases cured by eating properly."[17]

Carver blamed pellagra for the inefficiency of the southern black work force: "A sick, worried, rest-broken person cannot do his best either in the quantity or quality of the services he attempts to render." He called for black Southerners to "strike at the very root of the trouble, which is poor food."[18]

One food item that captured Carver's research interest early on was the cowpea, a lowly legume, high in protein and also known as the "blackeye" or "Southern" pea. In 1903, Carver published a bulletin simply titled "Cowpeas." In this publication, he extolled the virtues of the cowpea, explained how to grow it and what benefits it could provide as a soil enricher. He also described a variety of products that could be gleaned from it to benefit both humans and beasts. Carver's work with the cowpea, he wrote, was aimed at responding to "the demand for an increased quantity and better quality of nutritious forage for animals and a wider range of foodstuffs for man." He continued, "As a food for man, the cowpea should be to the South, what the White Soup, Navy or Boston bean is to the North, East and West, and it may be prepared in a sufficient number of ways to suit the most fastidious palate."[19]

Meanwhile, Carver transformed the annual agricultural conferences begun by Washington in 1892 into monthly "Institutes" held on the Tuskegee campus. Modeled after similar efforts that he had been exposed to at Iowa State, the Farmers' Institute that Carver launched in 1897 brought a regular flow of black farmers into contact with Carver, first from Macon County and later from other parts of Alabama and the South.[20]

A trip to Tuskegee allowed farmers to be exposed to Carver's magnetic personality and his enthusiasm for his subject. Carver was a showman, some might even say a "showoff." One man who fell under Carver's charm during a presentation later wrote to tell him, "You are the most seductive being I know, capable of making yourself loved by all the world when you choose."[21]

While at Tuskegee, also, farmers could see Carver's experiments firsthand. They could look at his experimental seed plots and not only listen to what he had to tell them about using natural fertilizers, such as the "muck" from the campus bog, or about the virtues of deep plowing, or the benefits of crop rotation, but also see the tangible results of those innovations.

Another benefit of attending the monthly Farmers' Institutes was that Carver would often distribute without charge high-quality seeds that he had obtained from the U.S. Department of Agriculture, often through the direct efforts of his old Iowa State mentor and current USDA secretary James A. Wilson. Without Carver's ability to obtain free seeds and to explain how and when to plant and care for them, many of these poorly educated African American agrarians would have had far less chance of achieving economic independence.[22]

Carver turned the farmers' conferences into family affairs by providing a reason for wives to attend. He showed the women his macramé and other "fancy work" and handed out recipes, explaining how to prepare meals that he had concocted through his so-called cookstove chemistry.[23]

Not every black family living in Macon County could afford the time and expense required to travel to Tuskegee for a farmers' conference. Nor could the poorly educated African Americans in the region who could not read learn from Carver's periodic bulletins.

In 1904, Booker Washington suggested that Carver remedy this shortcoming by "fitting up a wagon to serve as a traveling agricultural school." Carver responded with enthusiasm to the suggestion. On November 16, 1904, he wrote to Washington about how the wagon should be outfitted and even included a small sketch of its design.

Carver wanted a "light, strong wagon body for either a one or two-horse wagon made to open part way down, as per rough sketch." He wanted the wagon to be equipped with "a small milk separator, churn and complete outfit for making butter; at other time cheese." He wanted "large charts on soil building, orcharding, stock raising and all operations pertaining to the farm." Carver suggested "a young woman could accompany the wagon and give instruction in dairying, cheese making and poultry raising." He also advised Washington that seasonal demonstrations on canning, drying, pickling, and preserving fruits and vegetables could be offered, along with the preparation of "peas, tomatoes, cornbread and our common foodstuffs." And, he urged that the "traveling agricultural school" be prepared to teach farmers how to examine, prepare, and fertilize soils. Finally, he wanted farmers to be able to bring sick livestock to the wagon for consultation and treatment.[24]

The ever-resourceful Washington liked this idea, and he set out to find resources to furnish the traveling school. He persuaded Morris K. Jesup, a New York banker, to underwrite the cost of building and stocking the wagon, which became operational in the spring of 1906. By the end of that summer, more than two thousand people had been served by the so-called Jesup Agricultural Wagon. In the fall of that year,

Thomas M. Campbell, a former Carver student, was hired to operate the wagon, and the "traveling school" became part of the U.S. Department of Agriculture outreach program. Campbell thus became the first black demonstration agent. Campbell and the Jesup Wagon became fixtures in the rural Alabama countryside and contributed greatly to the practical education of many area black farmers.[25] As Booker T. Washington biographer Robert J. Norrell has pointed out, "During its first summer of use, the Jesup Wagon taught new techniques to more than 2,000 farmers in Alabama."[26]

Meanwhile, Carver had begun to host farmers' conferences beyond the Tuskegee campus, first in other parts of Alabama and then throughout the South. Irving Menafee, a Carver student who went to work at Voorhees College after leaving Tuskegee, reported, "It was largely through this agency [the annual farmers' conferences] that Professor Carver by reason of his food demonstrations became more generally known throughout the South." Menafee added, "He is considered the drawing card and his name attached to a placard or bulletin announcing a proposed farmers' conference will draw a larger number of interested individuals—both white and black—than the name of any other speaker." In part, Menafee asserted, this was because of Carver's total lack of pretension and his ability to identify with his audiences: "He is not only modest in disposition, but equally so in the matter of dress. His style of dress is simplicity itself. By a stranger he would very probably be taken to be some rural dweller or someone with a very limited training."[27]

Meanwhile, Carver's experiments with and thoughts about how best to renew southern soils continued to mature during the second decade of his tenure at Tuskegee. In 1905, he shared his conclusions with local farmers through an experiment station bulletin titled "How to Build Up Worn Out Soils."[28] He became an increasingly outspoken critic of the use of commercial fertilizers, in part because he knew that the farmers he sought to help could not afford them but also because he realized that those fertilizers offered no long-term help to the native soils.

Instead, Carver urged the use of "green" fertilizers, organic materials that could be added to the soil. In a letter to Booker T. Washington, Carver described some of the materials available on the Tuskegee campus: "decayed leaves, dead animals, decayed night soil, animal manures." The term "night soil" was a euphemism for human waste, deposited in outdoor toilets and in places where chamber pots were emptied. That Carver advocated the use of night soil for fertilizer evidences his commitment to the notion that he regarded no biodegradable matter as true waste.[29]

Despite his efforts to move black farmers away from total reliance on cotton production, Carver was pragmatic enough to realize that cotton would continue to be a major cash crop for all southern farmers for years to come. Hence, he sought to help them increase their yields while simultaneously reducing their production costs.

During his first decade of producing agricultural bulletins, Carver published three on cotton-related topics. The first came in 1899, Bulletin No. 3, titled "Fertilizer Experiments on Cotton." The second, "Cotton Growing on Sandy Soil," appeared in September 1905 and was, by Carver's own admission, "a continuation of [Bulletin] No. 6, on Soil Building." Carver began this bulletin with the assertion "that every acre of land in Alabama" could be used to grow cotton and, "could and should be made to produce at least one bale to the acre," even light, sandy soil that was the poorest in the state. The keys to profitable cotton production on poor or marginal land, according to Carver, were preparation of the soil, the use of "swamp muck, leaves, etc." as supplements to commercial fertilizers, the use of "good, clean [cotton] seed of a standard variety," and the "clean cultivation" of the crop to rid it of weeds and grass, all of which involved labor-intensive effort.[30] Three years later, Carver summed up his findings in a bulletin titled simply "How to Make Cotton Growing Pay" (1908).

In 1911, in a bulletin titled "Cotton Growing for Rural Schools," Carver proclaimed, "There is doubtless no plant more interesting to the casual observer, or more useful economically and more wonderful to the searcher for truth than the cotton plant." This time, he warned of the threat of the "Mexican Boll Weevil": "While it is true that the above insect is not in this county, it is nevertheless in the state, and is moving this way rapidly; so therefore we think it wise to call attention to the best methods of control up to date." The "best methods" suggested by Carver included 14 actions that could be taken by farmers, among them his seemingly "catchall" suggestion, "The rotation of crops and the use of legumes, peas, beans, vetches, etc."[31]

While these and others of Carver's many bulletins contained useful suggestions as to how African Americans could improve their material well-being, Carver sought to improve their lives in other ways, as well. For one thing, he found the drab, colorless cabins in which they lived depressing and stultifying. Aware that few if any of these rural residents could afford commercial paints or "washes" to brighten their surroundings, he sought to develop affordable coloring products from the native soils.

The result was a bulletin titled "White and Color Washing with Native Clays from Macon County, Alabama" (1911). This bulletin, like all the others produced by Carver, offered specific, detailed instructions on how produce a product, in this case, white and color "washes." Carver made it clear that his principal goal was "to aid the farmer in tidying up his premises, both in and outside, making his surroundings more healthful, more cheerful, and more beautiful, thus bringing a joy and a comfort into his home that he has not known heretofore, and practically at no expense."[32]

This bulletin followed on the heels of another, published two years earlier, that also aimed to help farmers spruce up and beautify their yards and gardens. Titled "Some Ornamental Plants of Macon County, Ala.," this bulletin listed a great variety of flowers, trees, shrubs, vines, grasses, and other "really beautiful and useful ornamental plants" native to the region that could add to the beauty of one's home, regardless of its size, design, or monetary value. Carver urged that "Every park and dooryard should contain just as many of these lovely native trees, vines, shrubs, etc., as fancy and good taste suggest."[33]

No doubt Carver's desire to brighten and beautify the modest homes of tenants, sharecroppers, farm laborers, and small landowners was genuine. One would expect no less of Carver the artist, as well as Carver the man, who sought to improve the lives of those living in "the lowlands of sorrow."

But there may well have been something else at play, as well. Carver seemingly believed, as did Booker T. Washington, that whites would judge blacks at least in part by the degree to which they seemed to imbibe white middle-class culture and values and mirrored middle-class behavior, nebulous as these concepts were. Even the "best" of blacks would be judged by the worst behavior of members of the race.

Carver's painting, or "brushwork" as he called it, was his primary means of artistic expression. He never abandoned teaching and research for art, as he once announced he planned to do, but he continued to paint into old age. (Courtesy of the Tuskegee University Archives)

Carver, it must be remembered, had been raised by whites and had lived among whites for much of his life prior to going to Tuskegee. In 1905, he graphically revealed his contempt for "lower class" blacks, who, he no doubt believed, were impeding the uplift of the entire race. Writing to his old friend Helen Milholland, he responded to an apparently disparaging comment about African Americans that someone had passed on to her. Carver distinguished between the behavior of lower-class blacks and others who were more refined: "Yes it is the 'dipo rats' ['depot rats'], 'livery stable', gangs and the general worthless class she has constantly come in contact with. The jentle [*sic*], refined, cultured, self sacrificing Negroes she sees but little of because they do not make themselves conspicuous."

Carver commented to Mrs. Milholland that "Slavery was a hard and terrible school" and that "we are a young race yet, not by any means perfect but every day and year marks a part or complete milestone upward." Then, in a comment that suggests his sense of separation from the black masses, he wistfully wrote, "Oh how I pray that the light may burst forth in all of its splendor upon such unfortunate people."[34] Similarly, on another occasion some years later, he wrote to another friend, commenting, "Wish so much as a race we would stop so much 'Jazz' and ragtime and turn our attention to more really worthwhile accomplishments."[35]

George Washington Carver, of course, saw himself as one of the forces that would help to bring forth the light into the lives of these "unfortunate people." In helping them to transform their lives and to focus on "really worthwhile accomplishments," he would help to transform the way in which whites saw both them and him. Biographer Robert J. Norrell has astutely observed of Booker T. Washington: "[He] knew that the vicious images of blacks had to be proved false by objective demonstration, not by mere verbal assertion. Blacks need to acquire land, wealth, skill, health, education, and sensitivity to beauty and order—the foundations of civilization and culture. Once blacks had demonstrated that they were civilized, their status would rise, and whites would accept them."[36]

Considered in this light, painting one's house and beautifying one's surroundings with ornamental plants took on new meaning. These were marks of civilization and refinement and were an important lesson to be learned, so important that Carver hoped "that every school-teacher will take pride in fitting up his school room in some one of the above combinations [of whitewashing or coloring], and will teach each pupil how to select the clay and prepare it."[37] This would constitute one of the many bursts of light needed to lift up an "unfortunate people."

NOTES

1. R. Douglas Hurt, "Introduction," *African American Life in the Rural South, 1900–1950* (Columbia: University of Missouri Press, 2003), 1.

2. Quoted in Robert J. Norrell, *Up from History: The Life of Booker T. Washington* (Cambridge, MA: Harvard University Press, 2009), 57.

3. Douglas A. Blackmon, *Slavery by Another Name: The Reenslavement of Black Americans from the Civil War to World War II* (New York: Doubleday, 2008).

4. Ibid., 195.

5. Allen Jones, "Improving Rural Life for Blacks: The Tuskegee Negro Farmers' Conference, 1892–1915," *Agricultural History* 65 (Spring 1991): 105.

6. Ibid., 108.

7. Quoted in Peter Duncan Burchard, *George Washington Carver; For His Time and Ours* (Washington, DC: National Park Service), 16.

8. Mark D. Hersey, "'My Work Is That of Conservation': The Environmental Vision of George Washington Carver," Ph.D. diss., University of Kansas, 2006, 146.

9. George Washington Carver, "Feeding Acorns," Tuskegee Experiment Station, Bulletin No. 1 (1898). All of the bulletins produced by George Washington Carver are available on Roll 46, frames 0002–0464, George Washington Carver Papers, microfilm edition, compiled and filmed by the National Historical Publication and Records Commission, 1975, Inman E. Page Library, Lincoln University, Jefferson City, MO.

10. Quoted in Hersey, "'My Work Is That of Conservation,'" 356.

11. George Washington Carver, "Experiments with Sweet Potatoes," Tuskegee Experiment Station, Bulletin No. 2 (1898).

12. Quoted in Burchard, *George Washington Carver*, 23.

13. Ibid., 20.

14. Booker T. Washington to George Washington Carver, March 20, 1912, Roll 5, frame 0061, George Washington Carver Papers, microfilm edition, compiled and filmed by the National Historical Publication and Records Commission, 1975, Inman E. Page Library, Lincoln University, Jefferson City, MO. Hereafter referred to as "GWC Papers." The original GWC papers are housed at the Tuskegee Institute Archives in Alabama.

15. Quoted in Roger L. Ransom and Richard Sutch, *One Kind of Freedom: The Economic Consequences of Emancipation* (New York: Cambridge University Press, 2001), 196.

16. Elizabeth W. Etheridge, *The Butterfly Caste: A Social History of Pellagra in the South* (Westport, CT: Greenwood, 1972), 4–5.

17. George Washington Carver, "Three Delicious Meals Every Day for the Farmer," Tuskegee Experiment Station, Bulletin No. 32 (1916), 5.

18. Ibid.

19. George Washington Carver, "Cowpeas," Tuskegee Experiment Station, Bulletin No. 5 (1903), 3–4.

20. Linda O. McMurry, *George Washington Carver: Scientist and Symbol* (New York: Oxford University Press, 1981), 117.

21. Quoted in ibid., 95.

22. Ibid., 51, 116.

23. Ibid., 131.

24. George Washington Carver to Booker T. Washington, November 16, 1904, GWC Papers, Roll 2, frame 1066.

25. McMurry, *George Washington Carver*, 125–27.

26. Norrell, *Up from History*, 366.

27. Quoted in draft of article written by Irving Menafee, enclosure in Menafee to George Washington Carver, April 12, 1918, GWC Papers, Roll 5, frames 1054–1057.

28. George Washington Carver, "How to Build Up Worn Out Soils," Tuskegee Experiment Station, Bulletin No. 6 (1905).

29. George Washington Carver to Booker T. Washington, January 26, 1911, GWC Papers, Roll 4, frames 1021–1022.

30. George Washington Carver, "Cotton Growing on Sandy Upland Soils," Tuskegee Experiment Station, Bulletin No. 7 (1905), 5–11.

31. George Washington Carver, "Cotton Growing for Rural Schools," Tuskegee Experiment Station, Bulletin No. 20 (1911), 5, 18–19.

32. George Washington Carver, "White and Color Washing with Native Clays from Macon County, Alabama," Tuskegee Experiment Station, Bulletin No. 21 (1911), unpaginated.

33. George Washington Carver, "Some Ornamental Plants of Macon County, Ala.," Tuskegee Experiment Station, Bulletin No. 16 (1909), 5.

34. Quoted in Gary R. Kremer, *George Washington Carver: In His Own Words* (Columbia: University of Missouri Press, 1987), 151–52.

35. George Washington Carver to Dr. M. L. Ross, June 28, 1931, GWC Papers, Roll 12, frame 1185.

36. Norrell, *Up from History*, 424–25.

37. Carver, "White and Color Washing with Native Clays from Macon County, Alabama."

Chapter 7

WORLD WAR I

This is an alarming situation.

—George Washington Carver, letter to Booker T. Washington

George Washington Carver's effort to produce foodstuffs abundantly and cheaply received a boost from the war-induced shortages that began to surface during the early days of World War I. The war began in Europe during the summer of 1914, in the wake of the June 28 assassination of Archduke Franz Ferdinand, heir to the throne of Austria-Hungary, by a Serbian nationalist. Although the United States did not officially enter war until nearly three years later, in April 1917, the war impacted Americans almost from the beginning. Shortages of food and manufactured goods began to appear throughout the United States during the early stages of the war.

Throughout the United States, governments at all levels urged increased agricultural production with greater efficiency and economy, while simultaneously reducing waste. It was a call that Carver had been making for years. His old friend from Winterset, Iowa, Helen Milholland, acknowledged as much in a letter to him during the war: "[I] suppose you are hearing and practicing conservation along all lines.

It is surely a lesson needed by many and will be long in the learning by some. But I think you and we will not find it excessively burdensome at least, for the present for we have so long practiced the saving habit."[1] Not surprisingly, Carver moved to respond to the challenges posed by the war.

On August 14, 1914, less than two months after the war began, Carver penned a note to Booker T. Washington, sending the principal "some suggestions I jotted down last night rather hastily along the lines I had in mind to be distributed among the farmers." The suggestions filled two pages and began with this stark and direct assertion: "Whatever may be the intensity or duration of the great European war, it has caused a tremendous drop in the price of cotton (unfortunately), our only money crop, while foodstuffs of all kinds bid fair to jump, as it were, skyward in price, leaving us to buy nearly everything we consume along this line, and nothing to sell. This is an alarming situation, and one that every farmer, gardner [sic], and family should face just as it is."

Carver's solution: "Every family having even a small plot of ground" should plant a garden and "by intelligent manipulation . . . raise enough vegetables to supply their needs." Those with larger plots of land could not only supply their own needs but also sell surplus produce.

Carver followed with a lengthy list of vegetables that could be grown, along with instructions on how to plant, care for, and harvest them. Finally, he offered suggestions as to how to preserve each kind of vegetable by "canning, preserving and drying."[2] The latter method, in fact, became especially important as wartime shortages of sugar and glass containers made it ever more difficult for "the humblest citizen" to can fruits and vegetables.[3]

Meanwhile, Tuskegee administrators sought to reduce the cost of feeding the school's faculty and students and wisely enlisted Carver's aid in the project. On August 24, 1914, Carver wrote to school treasurer Warren Logan in response to "our talk on the necessity of cutting down expenses." He offered suggestions that he believed "will result in the savings of several hundred dollars during the year," including detailed menus for breakfast, dinner, and supper that drew heavily upon earlier bulletins he had published on the sweet potato and the cow pea.[4]

Additionally, Washington apparently asked Carver to prepare an elaborate exhibit on foodstuffs that could be grown and produced locally, in Macon County. Carver began to work on the exhibit, but he found it difficult to complete the task while simultaneously carrying out a multitude of chores that Washington and others expected him to perform in addition to teaching his classes. Virtually everyone on campus seemed to expect Carver to do something, whether it was inspecting toilets; assessing the quality of food, grain, and seeds received; or examining starch used in the school laundry.

Finally, on Christmas Day 1914, Carver wrote to tell Washington, "I am very much behind with my work. . . . [It] is a physical impossibility for me to do all the work I am attempting and keep things going as they should." He asked the principal "that I be relieved of some of the things that others can do so that I can go ahead with this exhibit."[5]

Washington and others did try to reduce Carver's workload, if ever so slightly, in part because the principal wanted Carver to focus on reducing the school's food costs and in part because he wanted Carver to publish more bulletins that would aid farmers and others in adjusting to the economic challenges posed by the war.

Carver produced 11 bulletins during the war years, a period of productivity for him that was unmatched by any other three-year period of his Tuskegee employment. Among the first was "When, What, and How to Can and Preserve Fruits and Vegetables in the Home," published in 1915. It was an elaboration on the themes he had articulated in his letter to Washington the year before and began with this comment, "There is without doubt no activity connected with the farm or garden of greater importance than the canning and preserving of fruits and vegetables."[6]

Carver offered five arguments in support of this assertion. First, he wrote, canning and preserving are "the easiest, cheapest, quickest, and best method . . . by which we can have plenty of good, wholesome fruits and vegetables . . . when the fresh article is out of season." Second, drying and canning of fruits and vegetables preserved those "that otherwise would go to waste" because of a variety of deformities. Third, he asserted, "There is always a market for choice, home-canned goods, and many are the quarters, dimes, and nickels that can be taken in in this way." Fourth, he asserted that "It is a noticeable fact . . . that those who partake freely of fruits and vegetables every day have the clearest minds and the strongest and healthiest bodies." Finally, he avowed that, "With plenty of fruits and vegetables in the pantry or cellar, there is absolutely no excuse for suffering from hunger," adding, "It is astonishing how it cuts down the cost of living."[7]

Calls for this and other publications and the practical solutions they offered came from throughout the South and even beyond. A woman from East Feliciana Parish in Louisiana wrote to ask Carver for the bulletin "which treats of canning." She explained that she was "now on the field . . . canning for the Parish. We are sent out to can all the people can save for themselves during this high cost of living."[8]

Likewise, a county home demonstration agent in Opelika, Alabama, wrote to ask Carver for 100 copies "of your bulletin on peanuts," telling him, "[I] am using your recipes in my work. A state agent for rural schools in Raleigh, North Carolina, asked him for 25 more copies "of your leaflets on—[sic] Drying Fruits and Vegetables." Earlier, the agent had sent copies "to all our Home-Makers' Club Agents" but had run out and wanted more to send "to some others."[9]

Eugenia Taylor of Roanoke, Virginia, wanted the same bulletin. It had been recommended to her "as the best that can be had," and she was certain it would be helpful to her in her new job as "canning demonstrator in this city." A request came in from Carver's home state of Missouri, where Mabel Turner, dietician at State Hospital No. 3, in Nevada, Missouri, asked for "Bulletin No. 32 on subject of peanut" and also asked for information on soy beans. She stated the obvious: "The problem of foods certainly looms up large before the American nation at the present time." E. C. Saga, in faraway New York, wrote to ask Carver for a copy of his bulletin "Forty-Three Ways to Save the Wild Plum Crop" and complimented Carver by telling him, "If there is a food famine in this country, it cannot be laid to your charge."[10]

One consequence of the wide distribution of these bulletins was a dramatic increase in requests for Carver to appear in person at conferences and to give talks and demonstrations. A typical letter came in from a farmer in Pineland, South Carolina, who pleaded with him to visit his community for a farmers' association meeting later in the year so that Carver could "demonstrate to us your great and valuable aids in food production." The petitioner assured Carver that "the farmers all join me in this request and are venturing to look forward, with hope, for your visit to us." He then appealed to Carver's commitment to poor, black farmers by telling him, "You are aware Prof. Carver, how very much neglected our rural districts are; these great things that come about by genius are seldom enjoyed by a poor class of our own unfortunate people who are left to the themselves, apparently forgotten."[11]

Two days later, Carver received an invitation from the Northwest Institute, in Mansfield, Louisiana, asking him to address a farmers' conference and to deliver a commencement talk. The person inviting him gave assurance that "the leading people, both white and black are anxious to hear you and will aid in every way to make your visit here a great success."[12] Other invitations came from Columbus and Savannah, Georgia; Denmark, South Carolina; Utica and Tougaloo, Mississippi; Baton Rouge, Louisiana; Kansas City, Missouri; Frankfort, Kentucky; and many, many other places.

Although Carver tried to accept as many invitations to speak as possible, he could not accept them all. In late 1917, however, he received an invitation that he dared not decline: a request from U.S. Department of Agriculture officials in Washington to come to the nation's capital to demonstrate how to produce sweet potato flour and the ways in which it could be used to offset the critical war-induced shortage of wheat flour.

Carver's effort to produce sweet potato breakfast foods, flour, and other edibles had been going on for some time, given impetus by Booker T. Washington's constant demand that Carver come up with cheap substitutes for increasingly expensive and hard-to-get food items. Carver was inclined to try his products out on friends and acquaintances. An acquaintance in Washington, D.C., Augusta Rosenwald, wrote to tell him, "The sweet potato flour which you wanted me to try as a breakfast food came last evening, and I had it served to me this morning for my breakfast." Ms. Rosenwald's critique was direct and to the point: "I find that just by serving it alone with cream it becomes rather pasty and requires a great deal of cream." But, she added, "I tried also adding enough hot milk to make it of the consistency of cooked faring, and it has very much the appearance of Ralston's breakfast food. Then put a pinch of salt on it and served it with cream."[13]

The USDA and the Department of the Army were less discriminating in their assessment of Carver's sweet potato flour. Indeed, Carver could hardly contain his elation over the reception he received. As he reported it, "The Government decided that the sweet potato offered probably the greatest possibilities in the way of saving wheat flour of anything that had yet been discovered in America; they decided that the drying of the sweet potato was the most economical and had more good points about it in the matter of conservation, transportation, durability, ease of handling, than any other known way that had been discovered." According to Carver, the government planned "to test the thing and give to the Southern farmer a demonstration as to the advisability and wisdom of the encouragement of the drying of the sweet potato" by installing a "drier" that could process 100 bushels of sweet potatoes a day. Carver hoped to see this piece of equipment installed at Tuskegee Institute, although ultimately it was placed at Arlington Farm, Virginia.[14]

Although Carver failed to persuade the government to place its sweet potato drier at Tuskegee, his visit to Washington and the fact that his opinion was consulted and his research results solicited brought much favorable publicity for him and for Tuskegee Institute. As one friend who found out about this invitation wrote to tell him, "Your trip to Washington, D.C will mean more to our race than anything that has happened for several years."[15]

In 1918, Carver published "How to Make Sweet Potato Flour, Starch, Sugar Bread and Mock Cocoanut," a publication no doubt aimed at trying to address the shortage of wheat and wheat-based products that resulted from the war. In this publication, Carver explained how to make three different kinds of flour from sweet potatoes. "Flour No. 1" could be made from uncooked potatoes. "[A]ll that is necessary," he wrote, "is to wash, peel, and slice the potatoes real thin, dry in sun, oven or drier until the pieces are quite brittle, grind very fine in a clean coffee mill . . . or any type of mill that will make wheat flour . . . [and] bolt through fine cloth in the same way, [sic] as for other flours."[16]

"Flour No. 1," according to Carver, "is fine for making mock rye bread, ginger snaps, wafers, waffles, batter cakes, custards, pies, etc." He cautioned, however, that although this flour could be used to make bread, "it makes a dough deficient in elasticity, bread dark in color and a loaf that dries out quickly." Flour for "bread, cakes, pies, puddings, sauce, gravies, custards, etc." he suggested, should be made from potatoes that were first boiled or steamed, then dried and ground. For best results, he urged mixing this flour with wheat flour at a 1:3 or even a 1:2 ratio.[17]

Even when sweet potato flour was mixed with wheat flour, it dramatically extended the supply of the latter. Carver saw no limit to the uses that could be made of his sweet potato flour: "Here in the South and other sections of the country where fresh potatoes can be had almost or quite the year round . . . there are almost unlimited possibilities." He predicted that sweet potato flour "is destined to become more popular as fast as the public finds out what a delicious, appetizing and wholesome product these flours are."[18] A man in Seattle who read a newspaper article about Carver's making bread from sweet potatoes seemed to confirm this judgment. He wrote to Carver: "If it would not be too much trouble, I wish you would send me by parcel post or express about a half dozen loaves of this bread." He added, "I also would thank you to send me your booklet telling how to prepare the bread."[19]

Carver also had an impact on the war effort through his influence on his students while they were at Tuskegee. Many of them wrote to him during the war to tell him of their activities and contributions. P. B. Speer, a teacher in Atlanta, Georgia, who had spent three summers studying under Carver at Tuskegee, wrote to tell the professor how helpful that time with him had been: "I can see you busy teaching your enthusiastic classes daily now, in my mind, and oh! How I do wish I was there." Speer did not mention specifically the shortages engendered by World War I and America's decision to enter that war, in April 1917, but that is surely what he had in mind when he commented, "Never has there been such a demand for gardeners as now." He continued, echoing a theme that he had no doubt heard Carver preach many times, "We want now 'the greatest yield with least expense and injury to the soil.'" Speer emphasized that his time at Tuskegee "[h]elped me wonderfully" and expressed the wish that "every teacher could come to Tuskegee."[20]

Another of Carver's students had ended up in Braxton, Mississippi, where he found "County Demonstration Work" in "the little Piney Woods School." He wrote to tell the "Professor" that he had "worked day and night trying hard to strengthen them along the lines of farm-ing." He assured Carver, "The gospel of good farming has been con-tinuously preached and demonstrations given whenever possible" and further informed his old mentor that he had not used commercial fertil-izer and had no intention of doing so. The result: "The farm here . . . is considered by both races the best in the state."[21] M. L. Moore, another teacher who had studied under Carver, wrote to tell him of the war ef-fort being made by the 87 students of Cottage Grove, Alabama, school: "[We] have lots of things planted and growing. We are drying and can[n]ing at school every day." Likewise, J. D. Davis, who taught school at Columbus, Georgia, wrote to tell Carver, "We have created quite a spirit of gardening among the patrons and school children of our city, white & colored, or we are trying to do so." Davis told Carver he was having an "exhibition of home and school gardens and a mass meeting" at the courthouse the next month, and he expressed the hope that his old professor would attend and deliver the keynote address.[22]

Likewise, another former student, a young woman living in San Antonio, wrote to tell Carver all that she was doing to be more self-sufficient. "From the savings of grease from my kitchen," she wrote, "I have made one hundred and sixty pounds of soap." She kept a veg-etable and a flower garden and earned money by selling daisies for 25 cents per dozen. She made "all of my own toilet preperations [sic]" and sold what she did not use herself. At night, when she was not read-ing, she sewed, all of which, no doubt, pleased her former teacher.[23]

Alta Reed, a frequent Carver correspondent, wrote from faraway Roslindale, Massachusetts, to tell her former professor, "Your bulletins are so helpful, that it is hard to keep them." She told him she planned to go to Brunswick, Maine, soon, where she hoped, "to take charge of vegetables and berries at home."[24] Yet another former student, George White, wrote to tell Carver, "I have been composting manure, dirt, and leaves just like the one you have." He was having trouble persuading his father "not to buy any of the high price fertilizer," but he was mix-ing the commercial fertilizer with his composting material to "make the manure go further." George was physically unfit for military service, but he told the professor, "I think I can serve the government better by becoming a producer."[25]

Carver also nurtured the war effort by staying in touch with and encouraging former students who left the classroom behind to answer the call to service during World War I. Extant letters from soldiers to Carver often began with the writer thanking the professor for a recent piece of correspondence, a clear indication that these were two-way contacts. Such was the case with Ernest Frazier, who was stationed at Fort Des Moines in Iowa during the early days after America's entry into the war. On July 4, 1917, Frazier wrote to Carver, acknowledging receipt of "your most inspiring letter a few days ago." Something of the deep meaning of the war for African Americans in particular can be gleaned from Frazier's comment to Carver that "I am studying hard trying to make good for the whole race." Ten days later, in another letter to the professor, Frazier assured Carver, "If I should happen to go to France and fight for my country and race I shall gladly go, and die if needs be."[26] But another former student was less sanguine about the sacrifice he and others of his race were being asked to make. Writing to the professor only days after the East St. Louis Race Riot resulted in the deaths of numerous African Americans, he commented on the irony of fighting abroad for "my country" when members of his own race were being murdered in America: "I say my country but since that terrible affair in St. Louis I wonder if the negro has a country." The former student asked Carver, "What effect did the riot have on the Southern people," and then answered his own question by saying, "I suppose it is the same old story the negroes were to blame and it served them right."[27]

The riot that occurred in East St. Louis in 1917, of course, was one consequence of a massive movement of southern blacks to urban centers in the Midwest and the North. Known by historians as the "Great Migration," this movement witnessed African Americans abandoning their agricultural roots in the hope of finding good-paying factory and industrial jobs in cities such as St. Louis, Chicago, and Detroit.

But, as in the case of East St. Louis, black migrants challenged white workers for jobs and threatened to take up residence in what had been previously all-white enclaves. White violence was often the response. No doubt this threat of violence, unrest, and general racial clashing contributed to Carver's encouragement to blacks to remain in the South and continue their agrarian lifestyle, rather than abandoning their homeland for the North. Arguably, his clearest and strongest statements came in a personal letter to Dr. G. F. Peabody. Perhaps it was because he was writing to a white person, but Carver seemed to blame the lack of black initiative and black backwardness on the migrants, rather than on the oppressive racism of the urban whites they encountered. "I am not surprised at stupid and ignorant out-breaks," he wrote. "It seems perfectly natural to me that these people are congested in large numbers, subjected to an environment, wholly unlike any they have ever experienced before, and naturally many of them are not able to properly adjust themselves to their new conditions. Hence, they go off on a tangent." He continued: "I believe that the city or town where large numbers of these people congregate should institute carefully worked out control measures, such as would help them to properly adjust themselves to their new and strange environments. By so doing, the unfortunate outbreaks and racial troubles could be reduced to the minimum, and finally obliterated altogether."

Carver preferred that southern African Americans not leave the South for northern meccas. "I believe more strongly now than ever before," he continued, "that the south is the richest section of the whole United States, on account of the vast number of undeveloped resources, and I hope in the near future, we will become a great manufacturing section, as well as an improved agricultural, dairying, and stock-raising section." Were that to happen, "Many of these people would remain in the South and make fine factory laborers, but now we have no factories for them to go into." He concluded, "The work that I am trying to do has the above in mind and its goal."28

On another occasion, Carver complained that the Great Migration had been caused, in part, by the refusal of southern farmers to abandon their reliance on cotton as a cash crop, even in the wake of boll weevil infestations: "The coming of the Boll weevil in the South and the extraordinary wage inducements in the North and West began the unusual state of unrest, which meant of course, migration in large numbers." The solution, he believed, lay in "scientific investigation and demonstration." Black farmers could and must be persuaded to remain in the South.29

Although he seems not to have realized or at least acknowledged it, Carver's comments about the tendency of farmers to continue to rely on cotton as their cash crop more than two decades after he had begun to preach the gospel of diversification was a tacit acknowledgment that his message had failed to influence the majority of Southerners. Still, there is no denying that his World War I–era efforts had an effect.

It would be impossible to calculate just how many people Carver reached with his message of conservation and making do during the era of World War I. No doubt, the number was large as he reached out through his bulletins, his former students, and his speaking engagements. By the time the war was over, more people knew about him and his work than ever before. Nothing that had happened already, however, could compare to what lay ahead for him; the lowly peanut was about to make his name a household word.

NOTES

1. Mrs. Helen Milholland to George Washington Carver, November 11, 1917, Roll 5, frames 0912–0914, George Washington Carver Papers, microfilm edition, compiled and filmed by the National Historical Publication and Records Commission, 1975, Inman E. Page Library, Lincoln University, Jefferson City, MO. Hereafter referred to as "GWC Papers." The original GWC papers are housed at the Tuskegee Institute Archives in Alabama.

2. George Washington Carver to Booker T. Washington, August 14, 1914, GWC Papers, Roll 5, frame 0465.

3. Mark D. Hersey, "'My Work Is That of Conservation': The Environmental Vision of George Washington Carver," Ph.D. diss., University of Kansas, 2006, 302.

4. George Washington Carver to Warren Logan, August 24, 1914, GWC Papers, Roll 5, frames 0474–0478.

5. George Washington Carver to Booker T. Washington, December 25, 1914, GWC Papers, Roll 5, frames 0534–0535.

6. George Washington Carver, "When, What, and How to Can and Preserve Fruits and Vegetables in the Home," Tuskegee Experiment Station, Bulletin No. 26, (June 1915), 3. All of the bulletins produced

by George Washington Carver are available on Roll 46, frames 0002–0464, GWC Papers.

7. Ibid.

8. Bettie A. Planning to George Washington Carver, undated, probably 1917, GWC Papers, Roll 5, frame 0966.

9. Bessie Moore to George Washington Carver, January 17, 1917, GWC Papers, Roll 5, frame 0691; N.C. Newbold to George Washington Carver, June 2, 1917, GWC Papers, Roll 5, frame 0754.

10. Eugenia M. Taylor to George Washington Carver, July 14, 1917, GWC Papers, Roll 5, frame 0739; Mabel S. Tanner to George Washington Carver, June 13, 1917, GWC Papers, Roll 5, frame 0712; E.C. Saga to George Washington Carver, May 17, 1917, GWC Papers, Roll 5, 0700.

11. C.G. Bascomb to George Washington Carver, March 16, 1918, GWC Papers, Roll 5, frame 1030.

12. Byrd T. Crawford to George Washington Carver, March 18, 1918, GWC Papers, Roll 5, frame 1049.

13. Augusta N. Rosenwald to George Washington Carver, March 7, 1918, GWC Papers, Roll 5, frame 1041.

14. Quoted in draft of article, presumably written by Irving Menafee, enclosure, Menafee to George Washington Carver, April 12, 1918, GWC Papers, Roll 5, frame 1056–1057; Linda O. McMurry, *George Washington Carver: Scientist and Symbol* (New York: Oxford University Press, 1981), 169–70.

15. Martin A. Menafee to George Washington Carver, February 18, 1918, GWC Papers, Roll 5 frame 1010.

16. George Washington Carver, "How to Make Sweet Potato Flour, Starch, Sugar Bread and Mock Cocoanut," Tuskegee Experiment Station, Bulletin No. 37 (1918), 3.

17. Ibid., 3–4.

18. Ibid., 5.

19. Ernest W. [Illegible], to George Washington Carver, December 26, 1917, GWC Papers, Roll 5, frame 0955.

20. P.B. Speer to George Washington Carver, June 22, 1917, GWC Papers, Roll 5, frames 0722–0724.

21. [Illegible] to George Washington Carver, July 16, 1917, GWC Papers, Roll 5, frames 0748–0749.

22. M.L. Moore to George Washington Carver, July 24, 1917, GWC Papers, Roll 5, frame 0761; J.D. Davis to George Washington Carver, July 23, 1917, GWC Papers, Roll 5, frames 0758–0759.

23. A.O. Barns to George Washington Carver, July 16, 1917, GWC Papers, Roll 5, frame 0746.

24. Alta Reed to George Washington Carver, June 25, 1917, GWC Papers, Roll 5, frames 0726–0727.

25. George White to George Washington Carver, February 22, 1918, GWC Papers, Roll 5, frames 1017–1019.

26. Ernest Frazier to George Washington Carver, July 4, 14, 1917, GWC Papers, Roll 5, frames 0733 and 0740.

27. Oscar Parks to George Washington Carver, July 16, 1917, GWC Papers, Roll 5, 0750–0751.

28. Quoted in Gary R. Kremer, *George Washington Carver: In His Own Words* (Columbia: University of Missouri Press, 1987), 163–64.

29. Quoted in ibid., 114–16.

Chapter 8

THE PEANUT MAN

The peanut has become almost a universal diet for man.

—*George Washington Carver, "How to Grow the Peanut and 105 Ways of Preparing It for Human Consumption"*

George Washington Carver began experimenting with growing peanuts in 1903, seven years after he arrived at Tuskegee Institute. Initially, he was interested in the peanut because he thought it had great potential as a soil rejuvenator. Soon, however, he realized that the peanut could be used to supplement the protein-lacking diet of the black southern farm family. He began to explore peanut-based recipes that could be passed on and easily prepared.

A decade and more of research and experimentation resulted in the publication of "How to Grow the Peanut and 105 Ways of Preparing It for Human Consumption," published as Experiment Station Bulletin No. 31 in 1916. This 30-page bulletin began with Carver's assertion "Of all the money crops grown by Macon County [Alabama] farmers, perhaps there are none more promising than the peanut in its several varieties and their almost limitless possibilities."[1]

Carver praised the peanut for its soil-enriching capability, the ease and cheapness with which it could be grown, its value as a stock feed, and its nutritious value as a human foodstuff. "By reason of its superior food value," he wrote in the bulletin, "the peanut has become almost a universal diet for man, and when we learn its real value, I think I am perfectly safe in the assertion that it will not only become a prime essential in every well-balanced dietary, but a real necessity." He added, "I do not know of any one vegetable that has such a wide range of food possibilities either raw or cooked."[2]

In 1919, Carver reported to Tuskegee Institute president Robert Russa Moton that he had developed "a delicious and wholesome milk from peanuts." Somehow, Walter M. Grubbs, a representative of the Birmingham-based Peanut Products Corporation found out about this latest Carver discovery and traveled to Tuskegee to learn more about it. Carver wowed Grubbs, who began to publicize the black scientist's work.[3]

Eventually, George Washington Carver's experiments with and advocacy on behalf of the peanut brought him and his work to the attention of the United Peanut Growers' Association, a group that sought governmental protection against foreign competition for the peanut during the 1920s. The UPGA was only one of many organizations in the United States during that decade that sought to use the power of the federal government to eliminate international competition against their product.

In 1921, the powerful Ways and Means Committee of the U.S. House of Representatives held hearings on a proposed tariff that would protect American-grown peanuts against foreign competition. The UPGA asked Carver, the black scientist from all-black Tuskegee Institute in Alabama, to travel to Washington to make the case for the product and the industry.

It was, in retrospect, a most remarkable gamble whose outcome could in no way have been predicted. Would Carver, the unpretentious black man who often wore ill-fitting clothes and possessed what was sometimes described as an effeminate voice, even be allowed to speak to a congressional committee?

The decade of the 1920s was an era of racial unrest and hostility in America. Black migration out of the South during the World War I years brought thousands of African Americans to northern and Midwestern cities, where wartime factory jobs promised higher salaries than many Southern field hands had ever dreamed of. This Great Migration increased racial tension everywhere in America. White Southerners were angered by the loss of a cheap labor force and northern and Midwestern white urbanites feared black encroachment on their neighborhoods, their places of employment, and their way of life. Riots occurred in cities as diverse as Chicago and Tulsa, and the Ku Klux Klan revived and demonstrated new strength in cities as different as Denver and Indianapolis. The lynching of black men who whites thought acted as though they did not know "their place" reached epidemic proportions.

Given this racial tension, few Americans would have described a U.S. congressional hearing as a proper place for a southern black man during the early 1920s. There were no African Americans in Congress in 1921. Blacks held only menial jobs in the U.S. Capitol, and restrooms and eating facilities in the building were racially segregated, as was much else in the District of Columbia.

The hearing began with the committee chairman, Democrat Joseph W. Fordney of Michigan, telling Carver he would be allowed 10 minutes to make his case. The unflappable and confident Carver carefully removed a variety of peanut products from a carrying case, telling committee members, "I come from Tuskegee, Alabama. I am engaged in agricultural research work, and I have given some attention to the peanut, but not as much as I expect to give."[4]

Carver proceeded to show and talk about a variety of foods made from peanuts, doing so in a down-home, folksy manner that seemingly placed everyone at ease. Carver used humor, telling committee members that since they could not taste a peanut breakfast food, he would taste it for them.

He told them, also, of his work with the sweet potato and how "the peanut and the sweet potato are twin brothers and cannot and should not be separated," adding, "They are two of the greatest products that God has ever given us." He asserted, "If all of the other foodstuffs were destroyed—that is, vegetable foodstuffs were destroyed—a perfectly balanced ration with all of the nutriment in it could be made with the sweet potato and the peanut."

Early on in his testimony, Carver was interrupted by Congressman John Q. Tilmon of Connecticut, who delivered a clearly racial jibe in the form of a question: "Do you want a watermelon to go along with that?" Unruffled, Carver refused to respond in kind to a taunt. Rather, he stated matter-of-factly, "if you want a dessert, that comes in very well, but you know we can get along pretty well without dessert. The recent war has taught us that."

Carver proceeded to talk about making flour, coffee, and ice cream from peanuts. He talked about peanut-based foods for diabetics and also for livestock. He offered the prospect of dyes being made from peanuts. Aware that his time had probably run out, Carver commented that he should probably stop, but the chairman, charmed by Carver's message and manner, urged him on: "We will give you more time, Mr. Carver."

"Yes," affirmed Congressman John Garner of Texas, "I think this is very interesting. I think his time should be extended." Carver continued on, talking about the peanut, the sweet potato, about the chinaberry, about tariffs and the wisdom of using them to protect agricultural products. His time ran short again. This time the chairman surrendered completely: "Go ahead, brother. Your time is unlimited," he told Carver.

And Carver talked on, about milk made from peanuts and punches that, Carver assured the committee, did not violate the two-year-old Volstead Act, the nation's effort to implement a policy prohibiting the sale and consumption of alcoholic beverages. He talked about peanut-based oils and relishes. In the end, he fulfilled the prediction made by a peanut booster, who had told him on the eve of his appearance before Congress, "What you produce there will be one of the greatest advertisements for the peanut that has ever taken place. It will be an education and will acquaint people with Mr. Peanut more than anything else, as so few congressmen know anything at all about the peanut."[5]

When Carver finally finished his testimony, Chairman Fordney thanked him, and committee members praised him for his "great service," applauded his performance, and, interestingly, praised him for "the way you have handled your subject." He had accomplished a great deal in his 47-minute testimony before the House Ways and Means Committee. Most obviously, he had helped to secure tariff protection for American-grown peanuts. That protection was included in the Fordney-McCumber Tariff, passed by Congress in 1922 and named for the man who chaired the committee before which Carver had testified and Senate Finance Committee chairman Porter M. McCumber, a Republican from North Dakota. But he had done much more than that. He had made himself a spokesman for an industry, a folk hero who, ever after, would be identified with the peanut. J. M. Collum, a farmer from Putnam, Georgia, wrote to Carver soon after his appearance before the House Ways and Means Committee and prophetically summarized the significance of the event: "You have made this little thought of farm product [the peanut], famous, [sic] and it in turn will perpetuate your memory."[6]

African Americans throughout the South were delighted at the publicity Carver's testimony and the reporting of it drew—in a sense, he had made himself a role model for his race. Accolades poured in, including a letter from Tuskegee Institute principal Robert Russa Moton, who was traveling in New York but took time to write to Carver: "I just want to thank you again and tell you of the fine impression you made for the cause of Negro education and Tuskegee in particular as well as our race, in your splendid presentation in Washington." Moton added that he appreciated not only "the fine services you are rendering" but also "the modest, unassuming manner in which you do it."[7]

Similarly, Martin A. Menafee, a Tuskegee alumnus employed at the Voorhees Normal and Industrial School in Denmark, South Carolina, wrote to tell Carver that "we are all carried away with your trip to Washington. Seemingly, it has stirred up the whole country." Menafee told Carver, "our Banker [sic] paid you a very high compliment in the presence of several other white men in the bank yesterday morning." He added, "We are rejoicing as a race that we have such a man as you. We do not know how to appreciate your worth and value as you are a genius." Tellingly, Menafee told Carver, "Tuskegee has never appreciated your real value."[8] Meanwhile, back at Tuskegee, as if to refute Menafee's contention, the school's executive council asked Carver to present the "peanut exhibit" he showed the House Ways and Means Committee to the Tuskegee student body.[9]

The demand for Carver as a speaker increased dramatically in the wake of his 1921 congressional testimony, with many of the requests coming from whites and white institutions. It was a heady experience for Carver, the man who had never quite felt sufficiently appreciated at Tuskegee. Not surprisingly, he moved quickly to let people at Tuskegee know that he was in demand. On February 11, 1921, Carver wrote to tell Moton that he had just spoken at Alcorn College and that he was preparing to "leave by motor for Miss[issippi] College, located at Clinton[,] Miss." He emphasized that he would "address the white students," adding, "this is the most aristocratic college in the state so they say." He informed Moton that his appearance at the school came as a result of "a most earnest plea" from the school's principal, and that "They will send me by car to Tougaloo." From there, he planned to travel to Jackson, Mississippi, where he would meet the state geologist, "and a Journalist (white lady)," adding, "this is also by request." Likewise, he wrote Moton, the local Chamber of Commerce had asked him to address its members, but his busy schedule made that impossible: "will have to return later."[10]

The message was unmistakable: Carver wanted to let Moton and all his Tuskegee coworkers know that he was in demand elsewhere and that whites appreciated him and his work. Early in 1923, he accepted an invitation to speak at a white school in Atlanta. The courteous and attentive reception he received left him bubbling over with grateful, even boastful enthusiasm for days. He recounted the experience in a letter to a white friend: "It may be of interest to you to know that a special [railroad] car came from Atlanta . . . remained at the school [Tuskegee] twenty-four hours (24) waiting for me to get ready, took me to Atlanta, and remained there. . . . I lived on the car during a stay there. I think this is the first time in the history of the Negro race that such has happened." Like most African Americans living in the South during the 1920s, Carver was used to being treated like a second-class citizen. Riding in unclean, poorly kept, segregated railroad cars, being denied access to "whites-only" places of public accommodation, being forced to drink out of "colored-only" water fountains and using segregated restrooms—these were simply a way of life for black Southerners of Carver's era. Little wonder that he responded so positively to being treated as someone special. The nearly overwhelmed Carver commented, "I cannot help exclaim, 'what has God wrought?'" He added, "Throughout the entire visit, nothing but courtesies were extended."[11]

The warmth of the white response accorded Carver and his eagerness to nurture it made an experience he had at Tuskegee during the
summer of 1923 all the more trying and painful. The backdrop to the
controversy was the building of a new hospital for veterans in Tuskegee
to accommodate the needs of African American veterans, who were
widely recognized as being discriminated against at white VA hospitals
throughout the South. As historian Raymond Wolters summarized the
situation, "the nearly 400,000 Negroes who served in the American
armed forces [during the First World War] were barred from all but a few
wards in the government hospitals erected for disabled veterans."[12]

Initially, it appeared that the black hospital would be controlled and
administered by whites, but in the wake of Tuskegee principal Robert Russa Moton's ardent advocacy, President Warren G. Harding and
the VA administration agreed to allow the hospital to be run by black
administrators and black doctors. As George B. Christian, President
Harding's personal secretary expressed it, "It is the plan of the Director
of the Veterans Bureau, with the approval of the President, to man this
institution completely with a [sic] colored personnel.[13]

Whites in the town of Tuskegee were enraged by this decision, and
they sought to overturn it. Most, if not all, would have agreed with
the sentiment expressed by a white citizen who warned that the public
interest would not be served by placing African Americans in charge
of anything: "We who know the negroes know that you cannot put
them in charge or give them too much authority without their abuse
of same." He added, "A negro when given authority and backed by
the government will always abuse it."[14] State Senator R. H. Powell of
Alabama was even more direct: "We do not want any Government institution in Alabama with niggers in charge. White supremacy in this
state must be maintained at any cost, and we are not going to have any
niggers in the state whom we cannot control."[15]

Despite the efforts by Senator Powell and others to reverse the president's decision, the first of several African American administrators arrived at the Tuskegee Veterans Hospital during the summer of 1923.
Having failed to persuade governmental officials to reverse their decision, local whites turned their attention toward efforts at intimidating
Principal Moton and other Tuskegee Institute blacks, hoping thereby to
force them to abandon their effort to have the hospital run by African

Americans. Threats were made on Moton's life and against his wife and children. Additional threats were made against the black professionals who came to Tuskegee to take jobs in the hospital. When these threats failed, local whites arranged for a mass protest march by the Ku Klux Klan on the evening of July 3, 1923. A line of Klan supporters that stretched for two miles marched through the streets of the town of Tuskegee, while armed African Americans waited for the marchers to step onto the campus. A violent confrontation was avoided when Klan marchers failed to cross the campus, despite earlier threats to do so. Ironically, at least some of the marchers were white service workers employed at the hospital. After the march, they abandoned their hooded garments and went back to work at the hospital!

Controversy and conflict over this issue persisted for a year, leaving Carver hurt and confused. Many of the whites in Tuskegee who were among the most hostile critics of the effort to employ African American managers at the hospital were people he had regarded as his friends. Urged by other of his friends elsewhere in the South to flee Tuskegee for the safety of Atlanta, Carver felt compelled to remain with his black coworkers until the racial tension between town and campus subsided. The entire experience was an unwelcome reminder to him of the tenuousness and primacy of race in all things southern, regardless of his success and popularity.[16]

What impact did this experience have on Carver and on his relationship with and attitude toward whites and, indeed, toward his own people? A letter that he wrote to Dr. G. F. Peabody in the fall of 1923, only months after the July confrontation, evidences an unbridled obsequiousness toward whites in general and toward Peabody in particular. Moreover, in the letter, Carver went to great lengths to criticize the behavior of urban blacks who had left the South for northern cities and opined that they would have been better off in the South, despite the segregation and deprivation they experienced there.[17] This suggests that Carver wanted to avoid confrontation of the type that had occurred during the summer of 1923 and that the Veterans Hospital incident had redoubled his resolve to be more solicitous of whites and to take greater comfort from and pride in their statements and actions that affirmed him and his work.

A major opportunity for that kind of affirmation came late in 1923, in the form of the NAACP's decision to award him its prestigious

Spingarn Medal. This award was given annually to the African American considered to have "made the greatest contribution to the advancement of the race during the previous year."[18]

No doubt the publicity surrounding Carver's congressional testimony on behalf of the peanut made his a household name and nudged the NAACP forward in its decision to honor him. Carver was elated over the honor, seemingly in great part because it resulted in greater recognition and praise among whites. On October 8, 1923, he wrote a letter of thanks to Joel Spingarn, the white publisher and former NAACP board chairman, for whom the award was named. In the letter, Carver seemed to relish the publicity that came with his being awarded the medal, noting, "It is certainly having its own little effect right in our own little town." Tellingly, he remarked, "The white people seem to be even more anxious to see this letter than my own people."[19]

Carver wrote to his old Iowa State mentor, Louis H. Pammel, to tell him about the Spingarn Award and seemingly took the opportunity to lobby for an honorary doctorate from his alma mater, telling Pammel that such an honor would be even more important to him than the Spingarn Award. Pammel took up the idea but first inquired of Carver how he had come to be called "Doctor." Carver's response reveals much about his ability to seek praise and recognition while appearing to be modest and self-effacing.

He explained to Pammel, "The prefix 'Dr.' as attached to my name is a misnomer. I have no such degree." He blamed an accountant from New York City who had audited Tuskegee Institute's books during Carver's early years there: "He was greatly interested in my work, and said have you a Dr.'s degree. I said no. Well he said you ought to have it, your work really more than entitles you to it." Thereafter, the accountant called him "Doctor" Carver, "others took up the refrain," and Carver, at least as he told the story, was the helpless victim (or beneficiary) of well-intended praise: "I was powerless to stop it." Despite Pammel's support, the elusive honorary degree from Iowa State College never materialized. Instead, as biographer John Perry has written, "Simpson College gladly honored its most famous alumnus with an honorary doctorate. . . . In 1928, the college bestowed the award Carver longed for.[20]

Notoriety, however, brought scrutiny, and scrutiny sometimes led to criticisms of Carver and his methods. Arguably, the most painful such incident in Carver's life, certainly during the period after his testimony gave him widespread recognition, occurred in 1924. In November of that year, Carver delivered a lecture at the Marble Collegiate Church in New York City. As he had often done throughout his illustrious career, Carver took the occasion to attribute his success as a scientist to divine inspiration: "I never have to grope for methods: the method is revealed at the moment I am inspired to create something new." Human learning, he asserted, was of little value to him, adding, "No books ever go into my laboratory."[21]

Two days later, Carver and his methods were the topic of a very critical *New York Times* editorial titled "Men of Science Never Talk That Way." The editorial chastised Carver and affirmed the writer's conviction that his comments revealed "a complete lack of the scientific spirit," discrediting the scientist, the institution he represented, and, indeed, his entire race! Stung by the criticism, the prideful Carver penned a lengthy response, which provides insight into his methods, his thoughts, and his personality.[22]

Refusing to back down, Carver expressed regret that the writer of the editorial failed to understand what he meant by "divine inspiration." "Inspiration," he wrote, "is never at variance with information; in fact, the more information one has, the greater will be the inspiration." Criticized for relying on religion, Carver resorted to quoting scripture. He referred to "[St.] Paul, the great Scholar," and quoted lines from the latter's second letter to Timothy: "Study to show thyself approved unto God, a Workman that needeth not to be ashamed, rightly dividing the word of truth." Likewise, he turned to Paul's letter to the Galatians: "For I neither received it of man, neither was I taught it, but by the revelation of Jesus Christ."

Having restated his commitment to a belief in divine inspiration, however, Carver went on to chronicle his formal education at Simpson College and at the Iowa State College of Agriculture and Mechanical Arts and listed the names of dozens of renowned scientists whose work and writings had influenced him. He also informed the writer that he "receive[d] the leading scientific publications" and that he knew how to do science. Still, he retained his conviction that inspiration and revelation were critical elements of his scientific experimentation, and he continued to credit God with his success.

This incident and Carver's response to it reveal much about Carver, his methods, and his personality. Although he seemed to want to give God praise for his successes, he clearly wanted some human recognition for his accomplishments. He was deeply gratified by the large number of supportive letters he received from correspondents who wrote to tell him that they admired and agreed with his position. That many of his admirers were white seemed to please him even more.

In January 1925, for example, Carver wrote to Lyman Ward, the prominent white founder and principal of an industrial school in Camp Hill, Alabama. Ward had sent a letter of support earlier in the month, and Carver wrote to tell him that the letter had "lifted up my very soul." Carver told Ward that he had felt bad for a time after the appearance of the *Times* article, mainly because he saw it as "cynical criticism . . . directed at . . . the religion of Jesus Christ." Eventually, however, he claimed to see the criticism as a good thing, evidence "that after all God moves in a mysterious way His wonders to perform."[23]

A major consequence of the flap, Carver asserted, was that attention had been drawn to his cause, and interest in and support for his work had emerged as never before: "Since the criticism was made I have had dozens of books, papers, periodicals, magazines, personal letters from individuals in all walks of life." Additionally, Carver reported a dramatic increase in requests for him as a speaker: "I cannot think of filling ⅕ of the applications that are comeing [sic] in for talks." He added, "You may be interested to know that the greater part of my work is now among white colleges." Fiercely loyal to his way of doing science, Carver concluded by telling Ward, "I am not interested in science or anything else that leaves God out of it."

A major consequence of this conflict with the *New York Times* and of Carver's unwillingness to back down and his adamant advocacy of divine revelation as a source of knowledge was that, by the mid-1920s, the era that included the famous fight over the teaching of evolution that resulted in the Scopes trial in Tennessee in 1925, he emerged as a hero of evangelical Christians throughout the country. As historian Mark Hersey points out, "[Carver] was very warmly embraced by Christian publications, and . . . those publications played an important role in his rising popularity."[24]

One of the first of these publications was *The Golden Age*, published by the Watchtower Society from 1919 to 1937. In an article that appeared soon after the *New York Times* criticism of Carver, the author, Charles Henry West, defended Carver as "one of the few remaining true, honest and humble scientists of our day who are old-fashioned enough to still give God credit for the works of His hands." Presumably unaware that Carver had endorsed the writings of Charles Darwin in his senior thesis as a college student, West quoted Carver as saying, "I know that my Redeemer liveth. I know the source from whence my help comes. Inspiration, as I used the word in my New York lecture, means simply God speaking to man through the things He has created, permitting him to interpret correctly the purposes the Creator had in permitting them to come into existence."[25]

Publications such as *The Golden Age* and writers such as West laid the groundwork for similar works about Carver whose titles evidence their authors' emphasis on Carver's spirituality. Among these works are the following: J.H. Hunter, *Saint, Seer and Scientist: The Remarkable Story of George Washington Carver of Tuskegee, Alabama* (Toronto: Evangelical, 1939); Basil Miller, *God's Ebony Scientist* (Grand Rapids, Michigan: Zanderva, 1943); Alvin D. Smith, *George Washington Carver, a Man of God* (New York: Exposition Press, 1954); Yvonne Davy, *Mr. Creator's Borrowed Brown Hands* (Mountain View, California: Pacific Press, 1977); David Collins, *George Washington Carver: Man's Slave Becomes God's Scientist* (Fenton, Michigan: Mott Media, 1981); and John Perry, *Unshakable Faith: Booker T. Washington & George Washington Carver: A Biography* (Sisters, Oregon: Multnomah, 1999). Through the years, publications such as these did much more than Carver's peanut testimony to enhance the scientist's reputation beyond the campus of Tuskegee Institute, beyond the state of Alabama, indeed, beyond the South.

NOTES

1. George Washington Carver, "How to Grow the Peanut and 105 Ways of Preparing It for Human Consumption," Tuskegee Experiment Station, Bulletin No. 31 (1916), 3. All of the bulletins produced by George Washington Carver are available on Roll 46, frames 0002–0464, George Washington Carver Papers, microfilm edition, compiled

and filmed by the National Historical Publication and Records Commission, 1975, Inman E. Page Library, Lincoln University, Jefferson City, MO. The original GWC Papers and microfilm edition are housed at the Tuskegee Institute Archives in Alabama.

2. Ibid., 7.

3. Linda O. McMurry, *George Washington Carver: Scientist and Symbol* (New York: Oxford University Press, 1981), 171.

4. The transcript of Carver's testimony is reproduced in Gary R. Kremer, ed., *George Washington Carver: In His Own Words* (Columbia: University of Missouri Press, 1987), 103–13.

5. Quoted in Mark D. Hersey, " 'My Work Is That of Conservation': The Environmental Vision of George Washington Carver," Ph.D. diss., University of Kansas, 2006, 384.

6. J. M. Cullum to George Washington Carver, February 14, 1921, Roll 6, frame 0680, George Washington Carver Papers, microfilm edition, compiled and filmed by the National Historical Publication and Records Commission, 1975, Inman E. Page Library, Lincoln University, Jefferson City, MO. Hereafter referred to as "GWC Papers."

7. Robert Russa Moton to George Washington Carver, February 14, 1921, GWC Papers, Roll 6, frame 0672.

8. Martin A. Menafee to George Washington Carver, February 1, 1921, GWC Papers, Roll 6, frame 0671.

9. Secretary to the Principal to George Washington Carver, February 6, 1921, GWC Papers, Roll 6, frame 0676.

10. George Washington Carver to Robert Russa Moton, February 11, 1921, GWC Papers, Roll 6, frame 0678.

11. Quoted in Kremer, *George Washington Carver*, 164–65.

12. Raymond Wolters, *The New Negro on Campus: Black College Rebellions of the 1920s* (Princeton, NJ: Princeton University Press), 151.

13. Quoted in ibid., 161.

14. Quoted in ibid., 153.

15. Quoted in ibid., 163.

16. Ibid., 173–75.

17. Kremer, *George Washington Carver*, 163–64.

18. Ibid., 161–62.

19. Ibid., 162.

20. George Washington Carver to L. H. Pammel, November 26, 1926, GWC Papers, Roll 10, frames 0308–0309; John Perry, *Unshakable*

Faith: Booker T. Washington and George Washington Carver (Sisters, OR: Multnomah, 1999), 332.

21. "Dr. Carver Credits Genius to Divine Inspiration," *New York World*, November 19, 1924; Kremer, *George Washington Carver*, 128.

22. Kremer, *George Washington Carver*, 128–30.

23. Quoted in ibid., 130–31.

24. Hersey, "'My Work Is That of Conservation,'" 403.

25. Charles Henry East, "An Unscientific [?] Scientist," *The Golden Age*, GWC Papers, Roll 62, frame 0959.

Chapter 9

CARVER AND HIS BOYS

God gave you to me. . . . And oh how I thank Him for you, you came to me when I needed you most.

—George Washington Carver, letter to Jimmie Hardwick

George Washington Carver's new-found celebrity status, solidified by his testimony before the U.S. House Ways and Means Committee in 1921, had multiple consequences for the aging scientist. One result was that groups committed to promoting racial harmony in the South enlisted his help, and they paraded him before audiences of white youths, most of them male college students, in the hope that his presence and personality would have a healing effect upon them and upon American race relations.

In 1923, Will Alexander, director of the Commission on Interracial Cooperation, headquartered in Atlanta, invited Carver to address an annual conference of white Christian youths to be held at Blue Ridge, North Carolina. Ironically, the camp was headed by Willis D. Weatherford, whom Carver had encountered at a YMCA camp during the 1890s, when the two of them were still students. Back then, Weatherford questioned the propriety of involving a black person in an otherwise white event. As he wrote Carver many years later: "I was from a small college in Texas—yes, Texas—the state of wide prairies, but narrow prejudices at that time."[1] By 1923, however, Weatherford's racial sensibilities had softened, and he had come to think of Carver in very positive terms. He and others at Blue Ridge, for example, hoped that exposing white southern youths to middle-class blacks such as Carver would "begin to break down stereotypes and to foster a thoughtful approach to racial issues."[2] Even so, the Blue Ridge facility was not prepared to accommodate an African American guest, and Carver was forced into segregated facilities.

Despite the color barrier that pervaded the South during the 1920s and despite the initial Jim Crow reception he received at Blue Ridge, Carver received a warm response from the white youths he encountered. They, in turn, were impressed with his quiet and humble demeanor, his deep and expansive knowledge, and his palpable spirituality.

Among the first of the Blue Ridge boys to establish a relationship with Carver was a young man named Jimmie Hardwick, the eldest child of a Blacksburg, Virginia, merchant. Carver and Hardwick spoke to each other briefly after one of the scientist's early talks. Carver surprised Hardwick by asking the young man if he wanted to become one of "my boys." Startled by the question, Hardwick initially demurred. Later, he approached Carver, asking what he meant by that term. Carver responded that, although he had no biological children, he "adopted" earnest, intelligent young men who showed promise and possibility so that he could help them in their search for life's meaning.

Hardwick expressed the desire to join Carver's "family." Soon the young white Virginian, the descendant of slave owners, was corresponding regularly with the African American scientist, a former slave, who was more than three decades his senior. In late October 1923, Carver penned a powerful and poignant letter to his young follower. Although he began the letter with the salutation "My precious friend Mr. Hardwick," the familiarity and intimacy of the letter's message belied the salutation's formality.

Hardwick had written to Carver of his own personal spiritual struggles. Whatever the struggles were, they apparently kept Hardwick away from church, at least periodically. Carver responded with absolute understanding and unconditional support. He affirmed his Christian love for Hardwick, telling him, "I love you for what you are and what you hope to be through Christ Jesus." Remarkably, the aging Carver shared something of his own anxieties and frustrations with the youthful Hardwick: "There are times when I am surely tried and am compelled to hide away with Jesus for strength to overcome." In a hint of his frustration and disappointment at being underappreciated at Tuskegee, Carver told Hardwick, "God alone knows what I have suffered, in trying to do as best I could the job He has given me in trust to do, most of the time I had to work without the sympathy or support of those with whom I associated."[3]

This exchange between Carver and Hardwick, begun in 1923, continued for years. It is not surprising that a young teenager would transform the well-known scientist into a heroic figure worthy of adulation and be flattered by the latter's attentiveness and responsiveness. More surprising is the intensity of Carver's emotional attachment in this relationship. The affectation and raw emotion with which Carver poured out his feelings for Hardwick suggest the presence of a deep void in Carver's personal life. In 1923, also, Carver wrote to Hardwick, "God gave you to me for courage, strength, and to deepen and indelibly [sic] confirm my faith in humanity. And oh how I thank Him for you, you came to me when I needed you most."

Meanwhile, word of Carver's popularity as a speaker to YMCA groups reached the Atlanta office of the International Committee of Young Men's Christian Associations. In October 1924, the student secretary, J. W. Berthgold, wrote to tell Carver that he had "Several urgent requests for visits from you," including one for a six-college tour in North Carolina.[4]

Carver responded nine days later, telling Berthgold that the speaking tour might be possible, although he pointed out that Robert Russa Moton, the Tuskegee principal, had just embarked on a fund-raising campaign and that the committee appointed to seek funds "is planning to use me a great deal in their campaign work." Interestingly, to escape at least some of those fund-raising responsibilities, Carver encouraged Berthgold to "write a letter to Dr. Moton telling him something of the value of the work you want me to do in connection with the school and urge him to encourage my going as much as possible." Carver, practicing no little duplicity, encouraged Berthgold to avoid informing Moton that he had asked Berthgold to write to the principal: "you need not tell him that I have discussed it at all with you."[5]

As evidence of his popularity among "those dear Blue Ridge boys," Carver told Berthgold "that I have today received 115 letters" from them. No doubt at least one of those letters was from "the original Blue Ridge boy," Jimmie Hardwick. Hardwick visited Carver at Tuskegee during the winter of 1923–24. One is left to wonder for whom this visit must have seemed stranger: the descendant of slave owners or the descendants of slaves, living on the all-black Tuskegee Institute campus. On April 5, 1924, Carver wrote to Hardwick, telling him, "I studied you so closely when you were here and it made me very, very happy that I had the privilege of knowing you, and being able to call you a true friend in Christ." Later in the evening, Carver penned a "Postcript," in which he expressed gratitude to "my beloved friend Mr. Hardwick," for allowing him to speak so frankly: "I feel so happy that I know you, and can talk frankly to you as I do and that you do not consider my letters silly and foolish as they sound to me."[6]

Carver had long nurtured the notion of himself as being chosen by God to do special work, a theme he promoted to his boys. There is a confidence, even an arrogance, that permeates his letters, the kind of cockiness that often seems to characterize the self-promoting language of those who firmly believe that they are doing God's work and doing it well. In March 1928, Carver wrote to Hardwick, "O if you could right now step into 'God's little Work Shop' and see what He has permitted me to do, and its effect upon the south, you would marvel."[7]

Carver went on to tell Hardwick of the many ways God was using him, a listing of activities that strikes a modern reader as downright boastful. He told Hardwick, "Some days I do not do a thing during the entire day but entertain visitors. Ministers are coming as well as educators, five schools with their pupils have been here this year." More important than the visitors who came to Tuskegee, however, were the requests for Carver to go elsewhere. "Just think," he wrote to Hardwick, "of being asked to lecture before a group of Birmingham (Ala.) elite, Sponsored by the Birmingham Chamber, who had handsome invitation cards printed and sent out [to] about 1000 people." He added, "I spoke in the Empire Theater one of the City's finest." Perhaps most significant, Carver reported, "A number of prominent white people motored over to Birmingham, and took me there and back."

Upon his return to Tuskegee, Carver reported to Hardwick, he found waiting for him more requests for lectures. Ostensibly, Carver seemed to give God credit for the work He was doing through him. When Hardwick praised Carver's efforts, the latter responded, "No my friend the lovely things you say about me belong to God." Still, Carver wanted his young disciple to know of his many accomplishments and the great demand for his lectures and presentations. His letters seem like a cry for attention and acceptance, at a time (the 1920s and 1930s) and in a place (Alabama) where African Americans were still generally regarded as second-class citizens and denied full participation in the civil and political rights and privileges of citizenship.

Carver not only presented himself to Hardwick as someone who had been chosen by God to do wondrous things; he also encouraged his boys to think that they had been chosen. In one letter, he told Hardwick that he prayed regularly for him, telling him, "I never forget you, God has too big a Job for you to do."[8]

Hardwick continued his relationship with Carver into the next decade. Indeed, the friendship seems to have deepened with each passing year, reaching a new level of intimacy when Hardwick made another visit to Tuskegee in late 1930. As on other occasions, the two friends talked tirelessly and prayed intensely over several days. Soon after the visit, Carver sent Hardwick three lengthy letters over a three-week period, each of them articulating and elaborating on his vision of their relationship and the way in which it evidenced to him God's plan.

On January 5, 1931, Carver wrote to respond to the "marvelous letter" he had received from Hardwick. He told the young man, "God did indeed cause our paths to meet at Blue Ridge," adding, "you are the first boy he gave me." He drew a comparison between himself and the Apostle Paul, implying that Jimmie Hardwick and his other "boys" were to him as Timothy had been to Paul in the New Testament. He quoted from the book of Timothy, in which, he said, Paul referred to Timothy as "my son in the faith" and made reference to the need for Timothy to spread the good news of Jesus Christ after he was gone. So, too, Carver asserted, "Long after I have passed into the fullness of Joy, my dear little family of boys with their God-chosen colleagues must carry on, just as Paul's little Timothy did."

Carver reiterated the richness of the blessing that God had provided him by bringing Hardwick into his life and repeatedly thanked God for this gift. Reading these letters more than three-quarters of a century after they were written, one cannot help but feel that, in spite of Carver's references to the happiness that could be achieved by being close to God, Carver was an unhappy, lonely man who felt unappreciated and even victimized in the world in which he lived. He told Hardwick, for example, "I have to face so many prejudices and littlenesses that you do not have to contend with."[9]

For his part, Hardwick's commitment to Carver and his causes seems to have known no bounds. As the Great Depression settled in for a long haul during the early 1930s, Carver began to try to help those around him who had been adversely impacted by its consequences. In 1931, Jimmy Hardwick sent an undisclosed amount of money to help with the cause. Carver responded with effusive praise and gratitude for Hardwick and his action: "God will bless you in many, many ways for such a great heart. I was overcome myself, and I too thank you for more than my words can express." He encouraged Hardwick to believe "that this check is bread cast upon the waters and will return to you many fold. . . . [T]hrough this you are going to experience a new type of happiness."[10]

Carver not only became close friends with Jimmy Hardwick; he also befriended Hardwick's family. In 1931, he painted a small picture for Mrs. Hardwick and wrote to tell her that her son was "one of my greatest treasurers," adding, "the dear, handsome fellow is a constant comfort and inspiration to me." He sent Mrs. Hardwick seeds and rejoiced with her when they matured into flowers, all the while praising her son and expressing appreciation for his companionship.[11]

Hardwick was not the only young white Virginian to visit Carver at Tuskegee. John C. Crighton was another. Crighton met Carver while a student at Lynchburg College during the summer of 1923. Crighton was 19 years old, a native of Virginia, and a young man committed to the Social Gospel movement's effort to improve society through the wise and selfless application of the teaching of brotherly love to all human interaction. He was editor of the Lynchburg College student newspaper, an antiwar activist, and a member of the Christian Church, Disciples of Christ.

Crighton met Carver at a YMCA camp. In 1933, Crighton wrote to tell Carver, "It is impossible that I will ever forget our first meeting at Blue Ridge. . . . It was as if we stood in a wide landscape. You seemed to point to the distant horizon and ask, 'Do you see that towering range of mountains against the far horizon? You could climb those mountains if you tried.' . . . [S]ince our first meeting, you have been a constant influence in my life."[12] More than six decades after the event, he remembered Carver as being "fairly tall" and "very strong," "a very handsome man." Carver dressed plainly, often wearing "a black summer jacket, and a cap on his head." One of Crighton's most vivid memories of Carver was that he stayed up late, answering correspondence, but that he always rose early, "long before the rest of us got out of bed . . . he took a walk in the mountains . . . and he would come back with a small flower in his lapel . . . a very, very small flower. . . . It was representative of the total beauty of an actual world." When asked by Crighton and others why he took his early morning walks, Carver responded, "[T]o talk with God and the flowers."[13]

Carver invited Crighton to visit him at Tuskegee soon after the two met. Despite Crighton's Old South roots and the racial conventions of the time, he jumped at the chance to spend time with Carver. Likewise, Crighton's parents evidenced no anxiety about the prospect of their son going to the all-black school. Indeed, as Crighton remembered it many years later, his parents "were quite pleased and flattered that I would have as my friend a person as distinguished as Dr. Carver."

Crighton traveled by rail to the town of Tuskegee, where he was met at the train station by Carver, who walked with him back to campus. Carver had arranged for Crighton to stay in the "curators' quarters," rooms reserved for white members of the Board of Curators of Tuskegee Institute. His meals were prepared and served by advanced home economics students, a circumstance that allowed for the white Crighton and the black Carver to honor the southern tradition of racial segregation in a quiet, unobtrusive way. Crighton accompanied Carver on walks around the campus, where the scientist impressed the student with his sharp vision and his acute powers of observation. Crighton seemed at least mildly surprised by Carver's "somewhat distant relationship" to other campus residents.

Crighton visited Carver in his "apartment" in Rockefeller Hall, quarters he remembered as being "very Spartan. There was nothing ostentatious about it." The most notable feature was the presence of flowers, "particularly amaryllis, gorgeous amaryllis."

In a late-life interview, Crighton remembered how Carver would, among other things, invite his "boys" into his room in Rockefeller Hall and read to them. Crighton remembered in particular Carver's fondness for the works of the African American writer James Weldon Johnson. He recalled how Carver loved Johnson's 1927 book, *God's Trombones,* a collection of seven "Negro sermons in verse." Some six decades after Carver read the funeral oration to him, Crighton remembered "Go Down Death," the story of how God had commanded Death to go down to Savannah, Georgia, "down in Yamacraw," and rescue "sister Caroline" from a life of toil and drudgery.[14]

Like Jimmie Hardwick, Crighton became accustomed to being identified as one of Carver's "boys." He understood that Carver, a man who "had no family of his own," regarded his boys as "surrogate offspring" from whom he derived "a great deal of emotional satisfaction." Crighton also understood that Carver was preparing him and others "to carry on his work, to carry his message after he passed away."

Although Crighton visited Carver only twice at Tuskegee, the two men corresponded for a decade or more afterward. Crighton apprised Carver of his many activities, and Carver, in turn, responded "with praise and encouragement and satisfaction that one of his 'boys' was realizing the goal that he had envisioned for him." In one of his last letters to Carver, Crighton told him, "[Y]our confidence has been an inspiration to me t[o] translate my life's possibilities into reality . . . there have been few important decisions in which the thought, 'Would this please Dr. Carver,' has not carried weight."[15]

Yet another Blue Ridge boy who developed a close friendship with Carver was Howard Kester, a friend of Crighton's and a young man who led an effort to break down the racially segregated housing at the YMCA summer camp that forced Carver to sleep in a separate facility in 1923. Kester, too, maintained a long-time correspondence with Carver and visited him on multiple occasions at Tuskegee. While visiting Carver at Tuskegee, among other things, Kester allowed Carver to teach him how to paint with pastels, water colors, and oils. The two men also spent a considerable amount of time talking about how scientific agriculture could be used to improve the lives of poor Southerners, white and black.

By the late 1920s, Kester had become a leading voice in the Fellowship for Reconciliation for creating a southern center that would promote racial harmony. Carver wrote to him in 1929 to encourage this effort, telling Kester, "The beating on the tail of the snake may stop its progress a little, but the more vital parts must be struck before his poisonous death-dealing venom will be wiped out. Just so with the poisonous venom of prejudice and race hatred."[16]

No doubt Carver's words and actions influenced Kester in what would be a lifelong struggle for racial justice in the South. Indeed, in 1926, Kester credited Carver with being "the man who has been and is to this day the greatest inspiration in my life."[17]

Such adulation was common among Carver's boys. W. P. Nickell wrote to Carver from the YMCA Graduate School in Nashville in 1930. Referring to the professor as "My Dear, Dear Friend," Nickell told Carver, "you seem to understand, as well as to forgive[,] everything." He added, "One could not but love you for your infinite patience." Nickell summed up the reciprocity of the relationships between Carver and his young followers in this way: "I am sure that you must derive a great deal of joy from the visits of your boys, and what an inestimable joy and inspiration they must get!" He signed the letter "Your Boy" and affirmed his "Love and adoration always."[18]

Dana Johnson, a young man from Columbus, Georgia, was another of Carver's "boys," although the two met under somewhat different circumstances. Johnson's relationship with Carver stemmed, in part, from their mutual interest in art. Johnson's brother Cecil introduced Dana to Carver, whom Cecil had met during the summer of 1929 while working for the Tom Huston Peanut Company, a firm Carver was serving as a consultant. For months after meeting Carver, Cecil urged Dana to join him in a visit to Tuskegee, at the invitation of Carver. As Dana remembered it decades later, "[Cecil] had just fallen in love with him himself." Finally, on New Year's Day 1930, the two Georgia Tech students drove the 42 miles to Tuskegee to see Carver.[19]

Cecil and Dana Johnson walked into Carver's laboratory as sculptor Isabel Schultz was working on a bas relief of the scientist. Carver, who was working over a microscope, asked Dana what he thought of her work. Dana responded that he thought the nose was too large. Carver instantly took a liking to Dana Johnson and began talking with him about art, a field that Johnson was preparing to enter.

Their mutual interest in art made the bond between Dana Johnson and Carver especially close. Over the course of the next 13 years, until Carver's death in January 1943, Johnson and Carver corresponded frequently, and Johnson visited Carver often on the Tuskegee campus. During the first year of their relationship and at Carver's urging, Johnson sent him some sketches he had done so that Carver could critique them.

Carver responded with encouragement and nurturing, constructive criticism. He told Dana Johnson that all his sketches showed "marked ability" and then proceeded to comment on each one: "The shadows in No. 1 extend too far around for your ball to float out in air." Another of the sketches displayed "no middle distance or extreme distance[,] which are so essential to a pleasing picture." The foliage was too green: "it needs to be lightened up considerably by putting in shades and highlights." But two other sketches Johnson sent seemed to Carver to be above criticism. He told Johnson, "No. 2 has wonderful strength and character. . . . Your color schemes are rich and suggestive." Carver added, "I like this one, very much." Yet another of Johnson's pieces Carver labeled "very good indeed." He encouraged Johnson to "Do as much sketching as you can" and promised him that he would help Johnson with his technique when the latter came to visit him.[20]

The Johnson boys visited Carver at Tuskegee as often as they could arrange it. They welcomed being identified as "Carver's boys": "we just accepted it," Dana remembered, "that he was a very gracious and generous person and he was going to be a friend." As he did with John Crighton, Carver often took the young men into his "den," a somewhat cluttered room that prominently displayed a small spinning wheel that had once belonged to his mother. He told the boys that it was all he had left from his short life with her, and he touched it "with the greatest love and affection."[21]

Carver's den also contained book cases, "full jammed with books and pamphlets and magazines." Sometimes Carver would take a book out and "perhaps read a little bit of something scientific." More often, however, he would quiz the boys about their schoolwork and other activities and talk with them about their futures. "How you doing with your drawing," he would ask Dana, who often brought paintings with him for Carver to critique. "He was particularly anxious," Johnson remembered, "that if we did flowers or leaves or trees that I should be very accurate." When he was not, "[Dr. Carver] would correct me."

Sometimes Carver took his boys out collecting with him, and he would point out diseased plants, a wide variety of flowers, and various colors present in native Alabama clays. Dana Johnson credited Carver with getting him started in "the color chemistry work."

After Dana Johnson's graduation from Georgia Tech and a short sojourn teaching in a manual training school in Columbus, Georgia, Johnson landed a job "in the color chemistry business, manufacturing artists' material." Carver took a great interest in Johnson's work. Johnson, in turn, "would tell him of any new pigments that I had encountered.[22]

In 1933, Carver encouraged Johnson to continue his education at Columbia University's Teachers' College. Carver also took a great interest in Johnson's activities at a Methodist church in New York, and the two men spoke and corresponded about a variety of spiritual matters. Indeed, in hindsight, Johnson remembered, "[Dr. Carver] got me to thinking about [religion] even more than my parents." All told, Johnson estimated, Carver sent him approximately 100 letters during their 13-year friendship, which continued until Carver's death. Despite his extensive correspondence with hundreds, perhaps even thousands of people and his heavy research and speaking agendas, Carver sent Johnson roughly three letters for every one the much younger man wrote.

Dana Johnson idolized Carver. He regarded him as a master painter, once remarking that a still life painting Carver was working on was "the most beautiful thing I had ever seen." He regarded Carver as a mentor but also as a friend, and the bond that developed between the old man and his protégé obliterated the chasm that could have existed as a consequence of their age and racial differences.

For his part, Carver saw Dana Johnson and his brother as additions to his ever-growing family. In February 1932, shortly after a visit "from the two Johnson boys," Carver wrote to his "original" boy, Jimmie Hardwick, telling him, "[Dana and Cecil] are so wholesome and fine from every angle." He continued: "They are fitting into what we want so admirably." Carver thanked God "for the growth of our dear little family" and proclaimed its lofty purpose: "The only hope of the world as I see it."[23]

In 1932, the Commission on Interracial Cooperation invited Carver's "boys" to write letters to him, testifying to the meaning he had given to their lives and the value they placed on their relationship with him. Among the letters was one from Al Zissler, a young man who at the time had not yet met Carver and knew him only through the experiences of others and the letters he had received from Carver. That fact notwithstanding, Zissler proclaimed, "I am still your boy smiling thru." Zissler told Carver, "I have felt open to you in the beginning, not because of what you have accomplished, but because of the way you write." He added, "You just make me feel that I am one of your boys that wants to be of service to others. I am ever smiling and trying to help others."[24]

Howard Kester wrote to tell Carver that he was "thankful for that memorable day at Blue Ridge" when the two met: "Through your eyes I have looked out upon a new world of nature. Through your heart I have felt the heart throb of new races and nations. Through your mind I have laid hold of imperishable truths."[25]

No one, however, wrote a more heartfelt tribute than Carver's "original boy," Jim Hardwick: "You are so much a part of my life: are the object of so much of my thinking and affections that it is hard to imagine life without you."[26]

What are 21st-century Americans to make of these intimate relationships that transcended racial and generational differences and expressed themselves in such statements of love and commitment? Perhaps nothing more than the obvious: that George Washington Carver's ability to inspire and attract young people of good faith could not be constrained by the social conventions of his time and place. Carver's relationships with his boys, his letters to them, are powerful expressions of emotion from a deeply emotional man. The old professor, misunderstood by so many, found understanding, acceptance, and love in the company of and his correspondence with his young followers. They were Timothys all; he needed them to be that. It was the only way he could be their Paul. That role gave him strength in times of weakness, security when he felt threatened, satisfaction when he felt unappreciated. He needed his boys, and he needed them to need him. That mutual need, more than anything else, made his life and theirs worthwhile.

NOTES

1. Willis D. Weatherford to George Washington Carver, November 7, 1932, Roll 13, frame 1029, George Washington Carver Papers, microfilm edition, compiled and filmed by the National Historical Publication and Records Commission, 1975, Inman E. Page Library, Lincoln University, Jefferson City, MO. Hereafter referred to as "GWC Papers." The original GWC papers are housed at the Tuskegee Institute Archives in Alabama.

2. Robert F. Martin, *Howard Kester and the Struggle for Social Justice in the South, 1904–77*, Minds of the New South Series, edited by John Herbert Roper (Charlottesville: University Press of Virginia, 1991), 25–26.

3. Quoted in Gary R. Kremer, ed., *George Washington Carver: In His Own Words* (Columbia: University of Missouri Press, 1987), 172.

4. J.W. Berthgold to George Washington Carver, October 20, 1924, GWC Papers, Roll 8, frame 0366.

5. George Washington Carver to J.W. Berthgold, October 29, 1924, GWC Papers, Roll 8, frame 0386.

6. Quoted in Kremer, *George Washington Carver*, 174.

7. Quoted in ibid., 176.

8. Quoted in ibid., 176.

9. Quoted in ibid., 193.

10. Quoted in ibid., 178–79.

11. Quoted in ibid., 180.

12. John C. Crighton Jr. to George Washington Carver, February 4, 1933, GWC Papers, Roll 14, frames 0200–0201.

13. John C. Crighton interview, Kremer Interviews.

14. Ibid.

15. John C. Crighton Jr. to George Washington Carver, February 4, 1933, GWC Papers, Roll 14, frame 0200.

16. Quoted in Martin, *Howard Kester*, 39.

17. Ibid., 170n22.

18. W. P. Nickell to George Washington Carver, February 22, 1930, GWC Papers, Roll 12, frames 0024–0028.

19. Dana Johnson interview, Kremer Interviews.

20. Quoted in Kremer, *George Washington Carver*, 182–83.

21. Dana Johnson interview, Kremer Interviews.

22. Ibid.

23. George Washington Carver to "My great spiritual boy, Mr. Hardwick," February 1, 1932, GWC Papers, Roll 13, frame 0378.

24. Al Zissler to George Washington Carver, October 31, 1932, GWC Papers, Roll 13, frame 0986.

25. Howard Kester to George Washington Carver, November 2, 1932, GWC Papers, Roll 13, frame 1010.

26. Jim Hardwick to George Washington Carver, December 28, 1932, GWC Papers, Roll 13, frame 1255.

Chapter 10

SUFFERING HUMANITY

Our patients have usurped almost all of my spare time.

—George Washington Carver, letter to Mrs. Hardwick

Throughout his life, George Washington Carver believed that he could ward off diseases and treat those that could not be avoided by turning to the natural world. A proper diet was the first step in this process. In 1914, he wrote to Booker T. Washington to say, "There is probably no subject more important than the study of foods in relation to their nutrition and health. To understand them one must know them chemically, botanically, and dietetically." Carver told Washington, "I have not taken a pill, powder, salts, or oil as a purgative for at least 30 years. And it has been quite 35 years since I was in bed sick. I regulate myself with vegetables, fruits and wild herbs, Nature's remedies, which God intended we should use."[1]

On another occasion, many years later, Carver reported on a conversation he had with a farmer who had boasted to him of having a "good dinner" that "consisted of two large baked sweet potatoes." Carver's response: "I told him he did not have a good dinner . . . [that his meal] could not supply any of the vegetable salts found only in green leafy vegetables and which the body must have or the individual cannot think clearly or render a good day's work physically." Alternatively, Carver suggested the man eat "a good plate of dandelion greens . . . or a very rare dish composed of wild onions . . . [and then] he could have rightfully boasted of having a good dinner."[2]

Carver had never known a time when these kinds of "greens" were not a part of his diet. As a child, he remembered, "Never a spring came that we didn't have our wild greens. They were a part of our regular diet," adding, "They did indeed have distinct medicinal value. Our medicines before we learned how to make so many artificial products came from plants largely."[3]

Lessons from his childhood about how to treat diseases with plants and herbs abounded. In a late-life letter to the parents of a young Selma, Alabama, boy who had contracted whooping cough, Carver recalled what he had been told about how Moses and Susan Carver treated his case of the same disease when he was an infant: "I can remember the folks telling me that . . . they cured me with onion juice. That is, take a red onion and roast it before the fire until it is soft and squeeze the juice out of it and sweeten with sugar . . . or thick molasses. . . . This is a home remedy and has proven quite successful to my knowledge. . . . They tell me it saved my life."[4]

On another occasion, Carver wrote to a Mississippi woman about the medicinal value of nut grass: "As children, we ate the nuts as they are sweet and delicious in the Spring, and the plants have strong medicinal properties."[5] Likewise, he recalled, "We used to make syrup from the watermelon in our home when I was a boy." In another letter, he wrote, "The Water Melon, as well as other members of that group of plants are highly medicinal and suitable for certain troubles," among them stomach problems. Yet again, late in his life, Carver wrote to Henry Ford's secretary, telling him of the medicinal value of "sumac berries": "As far back as 170 years these berries were used for their medicinal and refreshing portions . . . especially valuable in throat infections, and certain types of stomach troubles." He recalled that when he was a boy, he and his playmates, including his brother, Jim, often made "sumac lemonade."[6]

Likewise, Carver learned at an early age to use the juice from plant stems and leaves as topical medicines. Writing to someone who had inquired about treating poison ivy, Carver acknowledged that some people used lime water, others strong soda water, but noted that Moses and Susan Carver's "favorite remedy was *Solanum nigrum* (black nightshade). You take the first leaves and stems, bruise them thoroughly, squeeze the juice out, and mix it half and half with sweet cream from cow's milk that is not soured and anoint with that." He added, "I have never known a case that it did not cure."[7]

The lessons Carver learned about the medicinal value of plants while a child in the home of Moses and Susan Carver were no doubt reinforced by his stay in the home of Andrew and Mariah Watkins during his adolescence and early teen years in Neosho, Missouri. In addition to serving the local community as a midwife, Mariah was widely known for her knowledge of herbal remedies and folk cures. She was one of the first people local residents turned to when illness or injury struck.[8]

Carver carried his knowledge of wild plants as both "foods and medicine" with him on his Midwest wanderings during the 1880s and early 1890s. For one thing, this practice helped him to live frugally, minimizing his need to purchase "groceries." Often he ate whatever he could find in nature, including nuts, berries, fruit, and wild greens of all kinds.

Soon after his arrival at Tuskegee, in 1896, Carver began to explore the plants of Macon County, Alabama, for their nutritional, medicinal, and therapeutic values. His eating of "wild" foods and his use of them for medicinal purposes became part of the Tuskegee lore. In 1916, Clement Richardson, a writer for the *Southern Workman* (Hampton Institute, Virginia) who visited Carver at Tuskegee, wrote of his encounter with the scientist: "There is the Carver who eats food for medicinal purposes—tomatoes for this, beans for that, rape for another trouble, cabbage for another, watercress for another, liquor of pine needles for colds, dandelions for something else." The amazed writer continued: "He knows and eats a score of vegetables that other people sneer at as weeds. He has a small range in his room, and when the bill of fare in the dining room is not to his liking or to the benefit of his health he goes out into the seemingly barren fields, brings in things (I have no better word), cooks and eats them, and is happy and healthy."[9]

At least one of Carver's former students remembered Carver's attempts at cooking in his room with less than fondness. In a late-life interview, she recalled passing by his room and noticing a noxious odor that permeated the area: "Dr. Carver's door was open. He was cooking something on a Bunsen burner. As I passed he said, 'Come in.' He was stirring up something. I looked at it. It seemed to have been some greens. . . . [He] said, 'taste it.' I tasted it. . . . It was all I could do not to make a face. It tasted terrible."[10]

At times he treated his guests to "weed sandwiches." One beneficiary of this experience described what happened: "Finally, [Dr. Carver] asked the time and announced that the time had arrived to make sandwiches. He then informed us that he did not know what was going into those sandwiches the day before but that night it all came to him in a dream. There the sandwiches were all spread out for him just as he should make them."[11]

On another occasion, Carver hosted the legendary automobile manufacturer Henry Ford and also served him a "weed sandwich." Later, he wrote to tell Ford the sandwich's ingredients: "The following things from Nature's garden formed the filling for the sandwiches you had for dinner: Curled dock (*Rumex Crispus*) tender leaves; Wild Onion (*Allium Canadensis*) whole plant; Chick Weed (*Stellaria media*) Whole plant when tender; Plantain (*Plantago major*) leaves; Pepper Grass (*Lepedium Virginicum*) young plants; Bed Straw (*Galium aparine*) tender tops; Dandelion (*Taxacum officinale*) young plants; Wild Lettuce (*Lactua Canadensis*) tender leaves; Rabbit Tobacco (*Anenaria plantaginfolia*) tender leaves and stems." Carver went on to tell Ford that on his next trip to the latter's Michigan home, "we will take your own dooryard plants and work them up."[12]

Carver even turned to the use of plants to treat Tuskegee Institute livestock, acting in his capacity as the school's erstwhile "veterinarian" in the absence of a formally trained animal doctor. In 1902, he wrote to Booker T. Washington's brother John, suggesting an herbal remedy for the school's dairy herd: "I would also recommend that once a month these animals be given a dose of condition powders made from various medicinal barks, roots, herbs, etc., which can be secured out of the woods and which forms the basis of condition powders." Appealing to Washington's ever-present concern about institutional costs, Carver emphasized, "This can be made here without any expense except the time and will be just as good as the condition powders we buy—in many respects better—because we will know the quantity and quality of the ingredients which enter into it." He added, "It would not be a bad idea to give all our stock a dose of these powders. In fact, the beef herd have been given theirs already. I am sure that if the above is carried out we will greatly decrease the number of deaths in the dairy herd."[13]

Eventually he identified more than 100 plants growing in Macon County that he believed had medicinal value. His greatest "discovery" of the medicinal value of a plant, however, stemmed from his experiments with peanuts and peanut oil. Initially, in the late 1910s or early 1920s, Carver began to develop a concoction of creosote combined with peanuts that was designed to be taken internally for respiratory problems. By 1922, Carver had named this product "Penol" and mentioned it and its curative powers in his speeches in many parts of the South. As Carver biographer Linda McMurry writes, "In a widely publicized New York speech [Carver] mentioned Penol and its great potential. A newspaper account implied that he had developed a new cure for tuberculosis."[14]

Throughout his life, Carver continued to research the medicinal powers of plants and to value their aesthetic qualities. (Courtesy of the Tuskegee University Archives)

Carver partnered with a local white man named Ernest Thompson to form the Carver Penol Company in the hope of transforming Penol into a marketing success. Penol did not become the commercial success that Carver hoped, and he soon developed a new medicinal use for peanut oil. He concluded that it could be used as a therapeutic massage oil to treat the lingering aftereffects of polio, especially in children.

Americans born after Jonas Salk's discovery of a vaccine that could prevent polio have no idea of the fear engendered by this dreaded disease during the first half of the 20th century. Known also as "infantile paralysis," polio seemed an especially cruel and quixotic threat to children of all ages and races. In 1908, researchers identified polio's cause as a viral infection, but no cure or preventive treatment for the disease emerged for more than four decades. Franklin Delano Roosevelt's contraction of the disease in 1921 brought added attention to polio in America, particularly after he emerged as the governor of New York in 1929 and as the Democratic Party's presidential nominee in 1932 and the nation's 32nd president the following year.

Although no cure for polio emerged prior to the 1950s, multiple researchers sought treatments for this disease that withered muscles, left its victims paralyzed, and even killed many of its less fortunate victims. Among the researchers who sought to treat polio and its effects was the Tuskegee agriculturalist George Washington Carver.

The genesis of Carver's belief that he could help polio victims stemmed from his observation that a peanut-based beauty cream that he developed seemed to give new vitality to the skin and muscles of those who used it. He concluded that peanut oil could rejuvenate limbs impacted by polio, especially if it was massaged effectively into the skin. Indeed, he seems to have believed that a good masseuse could cause peanut oil to actually enter the bloodstream, where it could have maximum impact, emphasizing that one "must not lay too much stress upon the efficacy of the oil alone, as its method of application has much to do with it."[15]

Carver's belief in the health benefits of massage stemmed from at least his student days at Iowa State College, where he performed massages for members of the school's football team. In a 1950s reminiscence written for an Iowa State alumni magazine by Burt German, one of the football players treated by Carver, German remembered the team masseuse "had almost a magic touch in those long fingers."[16] A firm believer in the benefits of a good massage, Carver continued to give massages to friends even after his arrival at Tuskegee.

In the mid-1920s, Carver began giving thrice-weekly peanut oil massages to 11-year-old Foy Thompson, the son of prominent white Tuskegee undertaker Cleveland Thompson and his wife, Annie Lee. Remembering the experience nearly a half-century later, Foy Thompson recalled that he had been frail, anemic, and underweight prior to being treated by Carver. After just 30 days of peanut oil massages, however, Thompson gained 31 pounds and achieved a new level of healthfulness he had never before experienced.[17]

Soon after his seeming success with Thompson, Carver apparently began providing peanut oil massages to infantile paralysis victims. He observed what he thought was unqualified success and began to nurture the notion that he was on the verge of a truly great medical breakthrough.

Despite his oft-uttered comments that he sought no personal gain or recognition for his "discovery," Carver simply could not keep quiet about his success. By the early 1930s, his speeches contained hints of his medical "breakthrough." A turning point occurred on November 2, 1933, when a Georgia newspaper carried a story about Carver's success with two infantile paralysis victims.[18]

Soon after, in late December 1933, T.M. Davenport of the Associated Press traveled to Tuskegee to interview Carver about his infantile paralysis work. Davenport reported on Carver's success: "After nine applications of the oil which was massaged into affected limbs, one of the subjects who had been walking with crutches was able to walk with the use of only a cane. The other boy less severely afflicted, had increased use of his leg and joined other boys in playing football."[19]

Davenport's AP article led to a groundswell of requests to Carver for assistance. Requests came in by the hundreds. Within less than one month of the appearance of Davenport's article, Carver had received more than one thousand requests for help. Scores of people, often parents with their diseased children, drove to Tuskegee to seek out Carver. He talked with parents and would-be patients, accepting many for treatment and turning many more away. Although he feigned frustration at having so much demand placed on his time and energy, Carver seems to have relished the attention he received. He also appears to have had no doubt in the efficacy of the treatments he provided.

In December 1934, he wrote to tell the mother of his young friend Jimmie Hardwick, "Our [sic] patients have usurped almost all of my spare time." He credited God with "contin[uing] to speak through the oils in a truly marvelous way." He told Hardwick, "I have patients who come to me on crutches, who are now walking 6 miles without tireing [sic], without either crutch or cane." In an account that strains credulity, Carver reported, "My last patient today was one of the sweetest little 5 year old boys, who 3 months ago they had to cary [sic] in my room, being paralyzed from the waist down. When I had finished the massage today, much to our astonishment he dressed himself and stood up and walked across the floor without any support."[20]

"Success" begat success and, no doubt, embellished its reporting. By the summer of 1936, Carver frequently reported to friends and potential patients that he had more than three thousand written requests for information and assistance. The staggering number of letters and pleas for help he received leaves one wondering how he even kept up with the correspondence, much less provided treatment or engaged in any of his research or lecturing responsibilities.

An exchange with a Gadsden, Alabama, parent in June 1936 reveals how heavy Carver's workload was and the lengths to which he was willing to go to help "suffering humanity." On June 9, 1936, Mr. A. F. Jones wrote to Carver, telling him, "For some time we have been reading with much interest the success you are having in treating infantile paralysis victims, with peanut oil." Jones proceeded to tell Carver about his young daughter, "who was stricken over five years ago," telling him that "we feel that your treatment would do her good." Jones, apparently an employee of the Nashville, Chattanooga & St. Louis Railway, asked Carver if he would see his daughter, suggesting that he could drive to Tuskegee and back in one day "by leaving early in the morning." He suggested visiting on a Sunday because he did not work on that day but made clear he would accommodate the busy Carver's schedule.[21]

Carver responded to Jones almost immediately. On June 12, 1936, he sent Jones information on "the oils with which I am working." In what was apparently part of his standard response, he told Jones, "I am not a medical doctor, and am not practicing medicine." Rather, he wrote, "I am simply a scientist looking for truth." He urged Jones to have his daughter examined by a physician, who, in turn, should "make out a chemical report as to the condition of the muscles involved, and send it to me." His work, he wrote, "is directly with the muscles, singling out each one and working directly upon it or indirectly as the case would warrant." He expressed the hope that he could advise on treatment through the mail but agreed to see the girl and her parents if treatment by letter did not work. Although he did not explain this to Mr. Jones, he declined to treat the girl directly, no doubt extending his policy of not massaging women even to young females.[22] Still, he said, if it became necessary "to bring the child down," he would "show the mother just how to handle the case." Carver expressed the intent to accommodate Jones's desire to visit on Sunday, even though he acknowledged that "Sunday is a very heavy day for me."[23]

Carver remained in touch with the patients he treated, writing letters of encouragement and offering advice. To Robert Thompson of East Tallassee, Alabama, he wrote, "I so thoroughly believe that by and by you are going to be walking again." Carver shared with Robert a biblical verse that he encouraged him to "constantly keep in mind": "In all thy ways acknowledge Him and He shall direct thy paths."

The Carver-Thompson correspondence reveals Carver's ability and propensity to view all human experience as the working out of God's will. Rather than emphasizing his patients' limitations, Carver encouraged them to search for God's meaning and purpose in their afflictions. He told Robert Thompson, "There are so many things that we cannot understand the why, and I so thoroughly believe in your case that as development goes on you will see the wisdom of a Great Creator in it all, as you will have so many experiences, learn so much that you could not possibly have learned had this not come upon you." Indeed, Carver went so far as to suggest that the time would come when Thompson would thank God for being afflicted with infantile paralysis because "it did stop something that might have led you to destruction and blighted your happiness in life." Instead, Carver preached, "I believe you are on the road to real happiness," adding, "it will be so thrilling from time to time to note life coming back into the lifeless limbs." Besides, Carver noted, "had this not come upon you, I would not have known my boy Robert, which means much to me."[24]

Whether it was the peanut oil massages, the healing faith that Carver inspired in his patients, or a combination of the two, many reported progress in their fight against the aftereffects of infantile paralysis. J.R. Caldwell, for example, wrote to Carver in June 1936 "to let you know my progress." He reported, "I am walking around in the house now assisted only by a crutch of course," adding, "I have to take it slow." Two months later, Caldwell excitedly wrote to tell Carver, "Thursday evening I felt my nerve coming back (the first time in two years)." Caldwell added, "It made me feel so good that I wanted you to know it. I felt that in my right arm."[25]

Carver's work on behalf of infantile paralysis victims and the publicity it generated brought a new level of interest in him and his work. In 1936, a *Reader's Digest* article about his work and the subsequent widespread distribution of a photograph of Carver working with an infantile paralysis victim led to even further demands for Carver's treatments.[26] At least one of his supporters, a medical doctor named L.C. Fischer, from Atlanta, Georgia, warned him against allowing "the lay press" to publicize his work. Such publicity, Dr. Fischer warned, "would destroy the wonderful effort you are making and certainly so far as it ever receiving any recognition or help from the medical profession."[27]

But Carver would not heed the doctor's advice. Whether he was motivated merely by an earnest and honest desire to relieve suffering, by the desire to see his efforts praised in print, or by a combination of the two, he continued to seek and respond to efforts to publicize his work. Indeed, he seems to have sought out the opportunity to treat the most famous polio victim in the country, the president of the United States, Franklin Delano Roosevelt. Carver hinted at and hoped for a request for treatment from the president. In 1938, with no request forthcoming, Carver sent Roosevelt a bottle of peanut oil. In 1939, Roosevelt actually visited Carver at Tuskegee, although the visit was so brief that the president did not even get out of his car. Nonetheless, the president's visit created quite a stir on the Tuskegee campus. A half-century later, Carver's coworkers still recalled with pride that the president of the United States thought enough of one of their own to visit the campus. A photograph of Carver leaning into the president's car to greet him, both men smiling as if they were old friends, circulated throughout the country and did much to enhance the Carver mystique. So, too, did a letter subsequently sent by the president to Carver, in which Roosevelt acknowledged, "I do use peanut oil from time to time and I am sure that it helps."[28]

Carver tried to parlay this type of endorsement and the publicity surrounding his work into greater support for his efforts. One of his most energetic promoters, James Hale Porter, tried unsuccessfully to get the National Foundation for Infantile Paralysis to provide financial support for Carver's treatments.[29] The fact is that, despite Carver's belief to the contrary, there was no scientific or medical support for his contention that his peanut oil massages had a beneficial impact on the patients he treated. And yet, there is no denying that interaction with the gentle, spiritually serene, upbeat professor left many of his patients feeling better.

Carver's patients trusted him to help them, a factor that may go far toward explaining whatever success his treatments enjoyed. The depth of this trust is revealed in a letter written to Carver by Grant Jones in late November 1935. As Jones remembered it, Carver treated him with massages, "From the middle of '31 until the beginning of the '33 school term." Jones could not recall "just how you offered to help me" but added, "because of my implicit faith in you and your work I was, and still am, more than gratefull [sic], and readily consented."

For more than a year, Jones remembered, he visited Carver in his Rockefeller Hall quarters. Carver massaged his right leg, "and the result was surprising to both of us." Although circumstances beyond Jones's control forced him to leave Tuskegee and abandon the peanut oil massages, more than four years later, he remembered Carver fondly and with great gratitude. He wanted Carver to know "the appreciation and thanks for your interest and efforts in my behalf are ever present, not just one day in the year but all of them." Jones continued, "Your faith in human nature has taught me to believe in myself more and more each day. I have loved ones who I want to make proud of me and with the lesson I get from you in addition to the faith in myself, I intend to achieve that end." He concluded, "Once again I want to thank you for the priceless good, physical and spiritual, that you have done for me."[30] Another Carver patient was more succinct: "Upon leaving your office I remarked to my wife that I could well conceive the fact that Jesus was a man of color after knowing you. Your spirit of deep humility moved me and has made me resolve to be a better man and to attempt to live more accurately the teachings and principles of the lowly Nazarene."[31] Comments such as these made all the long hours and all the hard work seem worthwhile, indeed.

NOTES

1. George Washington Carver to Booker T. Washington, July 27, 1914, Roll 5, frame 0454, George Washington Carver Papers, microfilm edition, compiled and filmed by the National Historical Publication and Records Commission, 1975, Inman E. Page Library, Lincoln University, Jefferson City, MO. Hereafter referred to as "GWC Papers." The original GWC papers are housed at the Tuskegee Institute Archives in Alabama.

2. George Washington Carver, "Choice Wild Vegetables Now," *Montgomery Advertiser*, February 14, 1940, GWC Papers, Roll 46, frame 0859.

3. George Washington Carver to Lyman Ward, February 19, 1940, GWC Papers, Roll 32, frame 1068.

4. Quoted in Peter Duncan Burchard, *George Washington Carver: For His Time and Ours* (Washington, DC: National Park Service, 2005), 68.

5. George Washington Carver to Mrs. J. S. Sinclair, July 3, 1942, GWC Papers, Roll 42, frame 0053.

6. Quoted in Burchard, *George Washington Carver*, 69–70.

7. George Washington Carver to A. Girouard, September 4, 1941, GWC Papers, Roll 38, frame 0687.

8. Linda O. McMurry, *George Washington Carver: Scientist and Symbol* (New York: Oxford University Press, 1981), 20, 131.

9. Clement Richardson, "A Man of Many Talents: George W. Carver of Tuskegee," *Southern Workman* (November 1916), 602, GWC Papers, Roll 59, frame 808.

10. Elva Howell interview, Kremer Interviews.

11. Quoted in Burchard, *George Washington Carver*, 71.

12. George Washington Carver to Henry Ford, March 23, 1942, GWC Papers, Roll 40, frames 0683–0684.

13. George Washington Carver to John H. Washington, October 6, 1902, GWC Papers, Roll 2, frames 0456–0459.

14. McMurry, *George Washington Carver*, 191–92.

15. George Washington Carver to T.L. Hoshall, August 14, 1935, GWC Papers, Roll 18, frame 0072.

16. Quoted in Mark D. Hersey, "'My Work Is That of Conservation': The Environmental Vision of George Washington Carver," Ph.D. diss., University of Kansas, 2006, 63n34.

17. McMurry, *George Washington Carver*, 242–43.

18. Ibid., 243.

19. Quoted in ibid., 244.

20. Quoted in Gary R. Kremer, *George Washington Carver: In His Own Words* (Columbia: University of Missouri Press, 1987), 145–46.

21. A.F. Jones to George Washington Carver, June 9, 1936, GWC Papers, Roll 19, frame 0049.

22. In response to an inquiry from Miss Anna L. Childress of McKengis, Tennessee, Carver wrote, "My personal work is confined to men only, for reasons that you well know." George Washington Carver to Anna L. Childress, June 5, 1936, GWC Papers, Roll 19, frame 0033.

23. George Washington Carver to A.F. Jones, June 12, 1936, GWC Papers, Roll 19, frame 0081.

24. George Washington Carver to Robert Thompson, August 8, 1936, GWC Papers, Roll 19, frame 0538.

25. J.R. Caldwell to George Washington Carver, June 6, 1936, GWC Papers, Roll 19, frame 0038; August 9, 1936, GWC Papers, Roll 19, frame 0540.

26. McMurry, *George Washington Carver*, 252.

27. L.C. Fischer to GWC, June 12, 1936, Roll 19, frame 0080.

28. Elva Howell interview, Kremer Interviews; McMurry, *George Washington Carver*, 252–53.

29. McMurry, *George Washington Carver*, 253–54.

30. Grant Jones to George Washington Carver, November 27, 1935, GWC Papers, Roll 18, frame 0572.

31. Quoted in McMurry, *George Washington Carver*, 254–55.

Chapter 11

DEALING WITH
THE GREAT DEPRESSION

Are we starving in the midst of plenty?

—George Washington Carver, "Are We Starving
in the Midst of Plenty? If So Why?"

Infantile paralysis was not the only problem George Washington
Carver tried to address during the late 1920s into the 1930s. Another
was the Great Depression, an economic downturn that engulfed the
entire world and threatened to destroy the American way of life. Although the Depression is generally thought to have begun with the
stock market crash of October 1929, the economic woes of American
farmers, including African Americans in the South, predated that
event by nearly a decade.

The death and destruction spawned by World War I dramatically
impacted postwar decision making and caused many Americans to
want to isolate themselves from European affairs. Convinced that
trading with the Europeans had helped draw the United States into
the war, many policymakers sought to use tariffs of the type advocated
by Carver in his 1921 peanut testimony before the House Ways and
Means Committee as a way of preventing foreign goods and the possibility of foreign entanglements from affecting the United States and

compromising American life. Critics labeled this approach "protectionism"; promoters of the idea responded that it was nothing more than commonsense patriotism.

Unfortunately for American farmers, they had reached a level of efficiency and productivity unparalleled in the history of the country. The advent of commercial fertilizers and advances in labor-saving mechanical devices, including the introduction of the tractor, were revolutionizing agriculture. But, when the United States stopped importing European manufactured goods, Europeans retaliated by buying far fewer American agricultural products. Once American markets were filled, there were simply no other places to sell the agricultural surpluses. The surpluses built up, the demand and the prices paid for agricultural products went down, and American farmers found themselves in a dangerous and unsustainable situation. Their problems were only exacerbated by the stock market crash. Businesses failed, factories stopped producing, and unprecedented millions of Americans lost their jobs, their savings, and their ability to earn a living.

Although there is no evidence that he ever did so, Carver might have responded to the Great Depression simply by saying, "I told you so." For a generation and more, he had been counseling all who would listen to become more self-sufficient, to live frugally, to seek to diversify their agricultural production, and to avoid waste at all cost. In truth, by the onset of the Great Depression, although Carver had been working to improve the lives of southern blacks for more than three decades and although he had published dozens of agricultural bulletins, taught hundreds, if not thousands, of students, and talked to countless individuals, his well-intentioned efforts had resulted in little change in the lives of the vast majority of African Americans in the region. As historian Mark Hersey has written, "it seems evident that in failing to employ Carver's suggestions as fully as they might have, black farmers reinforced their dependency on their landlords and contributed to the perpetuation of their cycle of debt."[1] African American sociologist Charles Johnson documented this reality in a study of black farm families in Macon County, Alabama, published in 1934.[2] Johnson concluded that African American farm laborers in the county were becoming more, rather than less, dependent upon white landowners for their wherewithal. The fatal flaw in Carver's message of self-help lay in his failure to recognize that the vast majority of African American agricultural workers in the region did not own their own land and that there was no incentive for them to increase their productivity or improve the land owned by someone else. Moreover, as Hersey has noted, the future of agricultural production in the South would tend toward the mechanization and industrialization of farming, "a transformation that would necessarily entail the large scale displacement of black tenants."[3]

The onset of the Depression forced many, many Americans to take a new look at Carver's advice and the lifestyle it promoted as they hunkered down to weather the financial storm that dominated more than a decade of the country's economic and social life. In late 1929 and early 1930, many, if not most, Americans, George Washington Carver among them, thought, or at least hoped, that the Depression would be short-lived. In the middle of the first Depression winter, less than four months after the stock market crash, Carver wrote to James Thorington of the Pinkard Investment Company of Montgomery, Alabama. He had just returned from a speaking trip that had taken him to Kansas, Oklahoma, and Texas. He commented, "I am very certain something in the way of relief will happen. . . . I believe we are going to get something going before a very great while."[4]

Three weeks later, he commented to a friend that people were complaining about their circumstances everywhere he went, particularly the cotton farmers: "[they] say they have never been in such bad condition." He expressed "the hope that when spring approaches increased improvement of the times will keep pace with it."[5]

But spring did not bring any improvement, and, by October 1930, nearly a year after the crash, Carver seemed to sense that a turnaround was not going to be as easy as he had first hoped. On October 2, 1930, he wrote to Steven Brown of Pickensville, Alabama. Conditions in the South were exacerbated by an unusual shortage of rainfall: "[During] these extreme panic times, it is difficult to say just what will be the outcome. I am sure that you have followed the papers and noted the report made by the investigators with reference to the many thousands of people that are now suffering on account of the drought and must have aid, as they have practically nothing."[6]

Carver continued to try to help the cotton farmers who were hopelessly dependent on the production of cotton as a cash crop, even as he also encouraged them to raise alternative crops. Writing to his friend Dr. M. L. Ross, he acknowledged, "The cotton growers have appealed to me for help, the staple is deteriorating very fast so that the spinners are refusing to buy a great many bales, the staple being so short that their machinery will not handle it." He added, "I have begun this investigation and am finding some wonderfully interesting things bearing upon it."[7]

Some policymakers called for a reduction in the production of cotton by reducing the amount of acreage devoted to that cash crop; the hope was that a reduction in the supply of cotton would lead to an increase in the price cotton farmers could earn. Carver opposed such a plan. He thought that "the abandonment of our cotton lands [is] not being well thought out." He continued: "I do not see anything but temporary relief in such a movement, with ruin and disaster following its wake. I doubt if any legislation will help a situation of this kind." Alternatively, he suggested that new uses and markets for cotton and other agricultural crops would have to be developed.[8]

Carver saw in the white planters' solicitation of his help an opportunity to improve race relations. Indeed, his private correspondence during the Depression decade reveals that issues of race and race relations were often in the forefront of his thoughts and that he projected the quality of his interaction with whites onto all members of his race. No doubt this attitude was informed and shaped by his work over the preceding decade with the Commission on Interracial Cooperation and his increased interaction with whites, including his "boys." He interpreted white solicitation of and kindness toward him as signs of improved race relations. He commented to Dr. Ross, "I am now visiting cotton farms also white people come and get me to look over their crop, are very tender and considerate of me, so that I believe it is doing much toward breaking down the color barrier and making it easier for the dear young people of my race who must carry on long after I have been called hence."[9]

In the fall of 1930, Carver headed out on a multistate speaking tour, preaching the gospel of conservation and making do. Before he left, he wrote to his good friend Dr. Ross, asking him, "Pray for me please that I may do the best thing possible for my race while on this trip."[10]

As was always the case, he was well received wherever he went. Upon his return to Tuskegee, he received a letter from a woman who had heard him speak at a church in Cleveland. She told him, "You don't know me but I am happy that I know you and that you are a member of our race." She added that Carver "made me proud of the fact that you are a Negro." Only days later, a friend in New York wrote to tell him, "A mother just told me yesterday that her little boy said that he wished to be a great man like Dr. Carver."[11]

In addition to trying to help cotton farmers produce larger and healthier crops of cotton, he continued to try to find ways to encourage them to produce alternative agricultural products. In late 1930, for example, he continued to try to find new markets for the peanut. He explored the possibility of making paper out of peanut hulls, telling a peanut industry representative, "It would be a great boon to the peanut industry if this can be done, and I believe it can."[12]

In one sense, the Depression was a godsend for Carver. It made him appear insightful, even clairvoyant, as people rushed to embrace the message he had been imparting since arriving at Tuskegee more than three decades earlier. For his part, Carver seems to have redoubled his effort to try to teach people, especially southern farmers, to be self-sufficient.

But he was getting older, he was suffering from "inflammatory rheumatism so that I can scarcely walk at all"; travel for him had become increasingly difficult. Already in 1927, he evidenced a bit of crankiness in explaining to his host the travel conditions he required: "Please have me do as little riding on the train at night as possible, as my strength will not stand sitting up all night in a day coach. If the distances [between speaking engagements] are far apart some one should go with me or be at the station wherever changes have to be made." He made this last request because "I carry rather heavy baggage and it is hard for me to handle alone."[13] By 1930, Carver refused to travel alone. Although he did not charge a speaking fee, he made it clear that "I only ask for my expenses, which include that of my traveling secretary, or some one who will accompany me there and back, as I have not the strength to travel alone."[14]

One positive result of the Depression, Carver hoped, would be that it would halt the exodus of southern blacks to northern cities. Indeed, early in 1931, he urged Southerners to go "Back to the Farm," calling for them to adopt this phrase as their mantra and seeing it as "The only slogan that will make a crisis like the present impossible."[15]

Carver's call to return to the farm emphasized a 12-point program, much of it a re-articulation of messages he had been preaching for a lifetime. It was, perhaps, his clearest call to the kind of self-sufficiency he had witnessed on Moses Carver's farm nearly a lifetime before. He urged farmers to "Make up your mind now to not only live from products raised on your farm, but always have a surplus to sell." Surprisingly, he called for them to raise cotton as a cash crop but also to plant good seed, care for the plants fastidiously, and "Follow only approved methods of fighting the boll-weevil."

He recognized that "Many farmers will be too poor to buy sufficient quantities of commercial fertilizers for their crops." As an alternative, he urged farmers to turn to the "decaying leaves of the forest and the rich sediment of the swamp" and to spend "every idle moment from now until planting time . . . in gathering up these fertilizers."

Carver urged farmers to "keep one or two good cows, proclaiming that "A good, well cared for cow is half of any family's living." Likewise, he called for farmers to keep gardens: "Under no circumstances should a farmer be without a good garden. Nothing will pay him better." He called for them to raise chickens, proclaiming that "A start of twelve good hens and one rooster, with a little care, will furnish all the eggs needed in the family, some meat and a surplus at times to exchange for clothing and other necessities."

Carver urged the growing and consumption of fruit and nuts and the substitution of nuts for meat in daily diets, as well as the raising of livestock, especially hogs: "No other animal converts into meat so much foodstuff that would otherwise go to waste." He called hogs "mortgage lifters," asserting, "There is a great demand for hogs at all times" and promised that "[they] will pay any farmer out of debt if he will give them a chance."

Carver also returned to another familiar theme, urging farmers to beautify their surroundings: "[this] increase[s] the value of property and encourage[s] the very best class of people to become your neighbors." Aware that the majority of African Americans living on southern farms were not landowners, he tried to persuade readers of the bulletin that his "suggestions apply to the renters and share croppers with equal force." After all, he wrote, "Every landlord prizes a farmer of this kind and encourages him in every way possible. Such an individual begets the confidence and respect of every one with whom he comes in contact, making it easy to get assistance when needed."[16] Still, convincing farm laborers to improve and beautify the landholdings of others remained an uphill battle.

Meanwhile, Carver's reputation had transcended the South, and even the United States. Early in 1931, the Soviet Union, likewise struggling with the effects of a worldwide depression, invited Carver to come to Russia to "stay at least six months to study agricultural possibilities and direct the cotton investigation." O. J. Golden of New York pressured Carver to accept the Soviet Union's invitation, telling him, among other things, "You owe it to your race."[17]

Flattered to be asked, Carver could not bring himself to leave his work at Tuskegee. Instead, he recommended a former student to take his place.[18] Among the work taking up Carver's time and interest was continued research and experimentation on peanuts during the early

Carver was photographed in his laboratory at Tuskegee in January 1940. Over the previous decade, he had become famous worldwide. (Associated Press)

years of the Depression. He focused especially on research related to peanut diseases, much of it done on behalf of the Tom Huston Peanut Company, headquartered in Columbus, Georgia. In gratitude for his work, Huston commissioned a sculptor, Isabel Schultz, to cast a bas relief of Carver's likeness for display in his factory.

Carver was overwhelmed by Huston's gesture, and wrote to tell him so on May 15, 1931: "I have been moving around half dazed and more or less speechless. I have been trying to find words with which to express myself. I am making absolutely no progress."[19] Subsequently, Carver wrote to his friend, Dr. Ross, urging him to "write a personal letter to Mr. Huston, thanking him for one of the most outstanding things that have come to mark the progress of the Negro race in many years." Tellingly, once again, Carver made no distinction between tribute paid him and the parallel progress he envisioned it implied for the race. He could not contain his hyperbole. Huston's gesture, he asserted, "is so significant that it is hard for us to grasp in its fullness. Think of it a bronze likeness, life size of a Negro to go up in his factory to give everyone passing through inspiration." Carver told Ross that Huston "is a southern man. . . . He will appreciate [your letter]." (Ross did write Huston). Carver concluded, "I think . . . many of our real worthwhile people ought to write to him in behalf of the race."[20]

In December 1931, with the Depression more than two years old, he penned a short essay titled, "Are We Starving in the Midst of Plenty? If So Why?" and sent it, along with a letter, to the editor of the *Peanut Journal*. Clearly written in direct response to the Depression, Carver began this piece by quoting from the book of Proverbs: "Much food is in the tillage of the poor, but there is that which is destroyed for want of judgment."[21]

In assessing the cause of the economic crisis facing America, Carver asserted, "We have become ninety-nine percent money mad. The method of living at home modestly and within our income, laying a little by systematically for the proverbial rainy day which is sure to come, can almost be listed among the lost arts." To illustrate his point, Carver recounted a recent trip to "a large city," where he "was entertained in a very luxuriant home of the latest style of architecture furnished with every modern convenience, a Lincoln car of the latest model." These riches and an abundance of food notwithstanding, "when the subject of making a little sacrifice in giving and receiving [Christmas] presents in favor of the vast hordes of the unemployed, they were not willing to do it, and showed very conclusively by their system of reasoning why they needed presents this year more than ever before."[22]

Carver was not immune to the suffering wrought by the Depression, but he refused to allow himself to become "money mad." In the early summer of 1931, the Tuskegee Bank, in which he had been depositing savings for nearly 35 years, closed its doors, one of hundreds of banks throughout the country to fail that year. Carver wrote a friend that "the depositors have been unable to get a single cent of their money." Always the optimist, Carver refused to dwell on his loss and focused instead on his good fortune: "I am thankful . . . that I am well and have a job, and will start over again." At Christmas that year, he urged his friends "not to send me any Christmas presents this year, but give it to someone in dire distress."[23]

In "Are We Starving in the Midst of Plenty?" Carver went on to argue that the previous summer had witnessed bumper crops of fruits and vegetables. Despite this rich harvest, "Many bushels rotted in the orchards . . . many families put up absolutely nothing for the winter. Their excuse being [they were] too poor to buy jars or cans." As an alternative, he suggested, they could and should have "dried" their produce.

He also took the occasion to offer the peanut as one solution to the food problem. In part, no doubt, he was trying to find a market, or at least a use, for what he described as a "billion pound crop of peanuts of good quality." He argued, "Taking the peanut pound for pound, I know of no other farm or garden, or field crop that contains as many digestible nutrients." Peanuts, he argued, could be added to every meal and could become a staple of the average American diet "in a way that will bring one hundred per cent nourishment, comfort and joy especially to the many thousands jobless, undernourished people within our borders doing the lions share in keeping the body in fit condition for work as soon as business picks up."[24]

Carver's writings and speaking engagements during the decade of the 1920s and into the early 1930s brought him great visibility and popularity, but nothing thus far in his life matched the attention he received in the wake of the appearance a biographical sketch published by the popular *American Magazine* in October 1932. Written by James

Saxon Childers, a journalist for the *Birmingham News*, the article was titled "A Boy Who Was Traded for a Horse." It traced Carver's life from his birth as "a slave child . . . without even a name," through his Midwestern wanderings, including his college career at Iowa State, to his career as a scientist at Tuskegee Institute, where, "he has been joyously at work with everyday things, making something out of nothing, or next to nothing."[25]

Nothing in Carver's experience up to that point did more to make him an iconic symbol of the American "can-do" spirit than the Childers essay. The Carver who emerged from the pages of the *American Magazine* article was a selfless servant of the common good who sought neither recompense nor acclaim for his contributions to the well-being of his fellow man. Childers presented Carver as the person who "has done more than any other living man to rehabilitate agriculture in the South." It was Childers's article that gave voice to a long-standing rumor, unsubstantiated but nurtured by Carver, that Thomas Edison, the "Wizard of Menlo Park," and others had tried to lure Carver away from Tuskegee with the promise of a six-figure salary. Carver declined the offers, in true hero fashion, because he felt needed at Tuskegee, "where," Childers wrote, "his meager salary is quickly consumed in anonymously paying the bills of worthy boys, both white and black, who are trying to get an education."

Carver was flooded with letters in the wake of the appearance of the article, all of them praising him as much for his good character as for what he had done. One of his "boys" wrote to tell him, "The article by Mr. Childers has created a considerable sensation." "Walter" told Carver that, as proud as he and the other "boys" were of his accomplishments, "it's what we see in your eyes and what we feel in your presence that endears us to you most." "Walter" focused especially on Carver's life "as an example of great and unselfish service and of renouncing the uncertain lures of money-getting." The world needed Carver, "Walter" asserted, "especially in times like these when fortunes are collapsing and men are sinking into the sloughs of despondency because their lives have been built upon such insubstantialities as wealth and power. . . . The world so needs the profound message that you are able to give it." "Walter" went on to tell Carver, "If I were writing an article about you, I think I would call you St. Francis of Tuskegee, for all the world knows St. Francis of Assisi to have been one who gave his whole life to the alleviation of people's spiritual difficulties, while your very life in everything you do is a litany of work for people, and all that you ask of them is that they make the best use of what you do for them."[26]

Similarly, J. T. Hamlin Jr., of Herb Juice-Penol Company, wrote to *American Magazine* to request permission to reprint the article. "Just at this time our country needs a great deal of stimulating literature of this nature," Hamlin wrote. "It will steer us out of the depression quicker than anything we have seen."[27]

On October 19, 1932, the article's author, James Saxon Childers, wrote to tell Carver that his paper, the *Birmingham News*, would be carrying another story about Carver in the magazine section of the next Sunday's paper. Childers flattered Carver while arguably damning his own paper by telling the scientist, "It might interest you to know that your pictures are the first pictures ever printed of a Negro in this paper—that is what we all think of you up here."[28]

For his part, Carver relished the attention that Childers's article focused on him. He wrote to his close friend Dr. M. L. Ross, "Letters are still pouring in as a result of the article in the magazine. . . . It is being read in the schools, preachers are taking their sermons off of it." And, as was often the case with Carver when he reported on praise that had come his way, he feigned surprise at the attention he was getting but only after repeating it: "I cannot for the life of me understand." Carver also repeated Childers's comment to him with obvious relish: "It is said that this is the first time this paper [the *Birmingham News*] has carried the picture of a Negro."[29]

Soon after the appearance of "A Boy Who Was Traded for a Horse," Carver tried again to offer a solution for a way out of the Depression. He penned an essay titled "Creative Thought and Action One of the Greatest Needs of the South," which appeared in the November 1932 issue of the *Peanut Journal*. He began this piece by proclaiming, "There have been but few if any periods in the world's history that required more conservative constructive thinking and acting than the chaotic condition through which we are passing."

Carver, the old teacher who had always encouraged his students to take up new ways of thinking and to challenge the status quo, argued the need for stimulating and encouraging creative thought. "One of the greatest needs at the present time is along the line of food stuffs," he wrote. "Many and varied are the schemes and menus gotten up to fill the empty dinner pail of the countless thousands who are virtually in bread lines." He expressed amazement that no one was recommending using nuts to supplement or even supplant existing diets. "Now is the time," he urged, "for the application of creative thought in relation to the way it affects the food and commercial value of two of the most outstanding crops of the South—viz [sic] the peanut and the pecan."

He especially urged scientists and dietitians to take on the pecan and to think of new ways to use it in much the same way that he had already done with the peanut. "This great crop with its almost unlimited possibilities will soon be a commercial nonentity unless the creative research workers take hold of it. The pecan could and should be made the King of Nuts, just as the peanut (which is not a nut) is being made the King of legumes."[30]

Carver's contribution to the effort waged to deal with the Great Depression came in two forms. He offered practical, usable advice on how to produce alternative food supplies, how to create new and larger markets for agricultural products, and how to conserve scarce resources. But he also offered Americans an alternative way to interact with the world—a way to escape the "money madness" that he and others thought had brought on the Depression in the first place. As the Depression deepened during the second half of the decade of the 1930s, Carver continued to advocate the kind of "creative thought" that he believed held the key to the future.

NOTES

1. Mark D. Hersey, "'My Work Is That of Conservation': The Environmental Vision of George Washington Carver," Ph.D. diss., University of Kansas, 2006, 455.

2. Charles S. Johnson, *Shadow of the Plantation* (Illinois: University of Chicago Press, 1934).

3. Hersey, "'My Work Is That of Conservation,'" 457–59.

4. James Thorington to George Washington Carver, February 18, 1930, Roll 12, frame 0011, George Washington Carver Papers, microfilm edition, compiled and filmed by the National Historical Publication and Records Commission, 1975, Inman E. Page Library, Lincoln University, Jefferson City, MO. Hereafter referred to as "GWC Papers."

The original GWC papers are housed at the Tuskegee Institute Archives in Alabama.

5. George Washington Carver to Mr. Crawford, March 6, 1930, Roll 12, GWC Papers, frame 0045.

6. George Washington Carver to Steven Brown, October 2, 1930, GWC Papers, Roll 12, frame 0408.

7. George Washington Carver to Dr. M. L. Ross, October 1, 1930, GWC Papers, Roll 12, frame 0403.

8. George Washington Carver to Jack Thorington, September 11, 1931, GWC Papers, Roll 13, frames 0015–0016.

9. George Washington Carver to Dr. M. L. Ross, October 1, 1930, GWC Papers, Roll 12, frame 0403.

10. George Washington Carver to M. L. Ross, November 3, 1930, GWC Papers, Roll 12, frame 0486.

11. Jane E. Hunter to George Washington Carver, November 27, 1930, GWC Papers, Roll 12, frame 0506; Fred S. A. Johnson to George Washington Carver, December 6, 1930, GWC Papers, Roll 12, frame 0539.

12. George Washington to Bob Barry, October 26, 1930, GWC Papers, Roll 12, frame 0463.

13. George Washington Carver to Blake W. Godfrey, January 9, 1927, GWC Papers, Roll 10, frame 0504.

14. George Washington Carver to T. M. Patton, December 13, 1930, GWC Papers, Roll 12, frame 0558.

15. George Washington Carver, "Back to the Farm," unpublished, enclosure with George Washington Carver to Asa Vaughn, January 21, 1931, GWC Papers, Roll 12, frames 0703–0709.

16. Ibid.

17. O. J. Golden to George Washington Carver, April 18, 1931, GWC Papers, Roll 12, frame 0973.

18. George Washington Carver to John Sutton, January 26, 1931, GWC Papers, Roll 12, frame 0731.

19. George Washington Carver to Tom Huston, May 15, 1931, GWC Papers, Roll 12, frame 1018.

20. George Washington Carver to M. L. Ross, June 28, 1931, GWC Papers, Roll 12, frames 1184–1186.

21. Quoted in Gary R. Kremer, ed., *George Washington Carver: In His Own Words* (Columbia: University of Missouri Press, 1987), 117–19.

22. Ibid.

23. Carver to My dear Miss Chisholm, December 12, 1931, GWC Papers, Roll 13, frame 0221.

24. Quoted in Kremer, *George Washington Carver*, 119.

25. James Saxon Childers, "A Boy Who Was Traded for a Horse: The Story of Doctor Carver, of Tuskegee Institute," *American Magazine* 114 (October 1932): 24–25, 112–16.

26. "Walter" to George Washington Carver, October 7, 1932, GWC Papers, Roll 13, frame 0803.

27. J. T. Hamlin Jr. to Mabel Harding, October 20, 1932, GWC Papers, Roll 13, frame 0919.

28. James Saxon Childers to George Washington Carver, October 19, 1932, GWC Papers, Roll 13, frame 0896.

29. George Washington Carver to M. L. Ross, October 23, 1932, GWC Papers, Roll 13, frames 0937–0938.

30. Quoted in Kremer, *George Washington Carver*, 120–24.

Chapter 12

THE FINAL YEARS

There will come a day when, out of the soil, we will make our houses, our clothes, our automobiles—everything on earth we need.

—*George Washington Carver to Malcolm W. Bingay,*
Detroit Free Press, *January 7, 1943*

George Washington Carver published three new bulletins during the decade of the Depression, one in 1935 and two more in 1936. All were aimed at helping farmers and farm families get through the Depression, and all picked up on themes that Carver had developed much earlier in his career. It was as if the Depression and the austere conditions associated with it reminded him of why he had come to Tuskegee in the first place and called him back to his original purpose.

In October 1935, he produced "The Raising of Hogs," an elaboration on a theme he had written about a few years earlier. Interestingly, he subtitled this bulletin "One of the Best Ways to Fill the Empty Dinner Pail."[1] In this publication, Carver cited the high cost of sugar-cured hams, bacon, and lard and urged farmers to raise their own pork supplies. Once again, he asserted the need for "Every farmer to realize that the hog is one of the best mortgage lifters on the farm, and can be quickly and easily raised with but little or no cash outlay."[2]

Carver wanted farmers to raise pork not only for their own consumption but also for the market. He urged them to start by selecting a good breed—he wrote that he preferred Berkshires, not recognizing, it must be pointed out, that many farm laborers could not afford to buy a pure-bred hog. Next, he wrote briefly about housing that hogs required and then spent a considerable amount of space describing foodstuffs that could be used to feed hogs at minimal expense, reminding his readers, "Hogs are great scavengers, [able to convert] into meat much of the waste from the kitchen, farm, garden, orchard, dairy, etc."

Carver suggested a wide variety of "Native Foods" that could be fed to hogs, including wild primrose, lamb's quarters, wild plums, acorns, beech nuts, nut grass, and purslane. Additionally, he proposed more than half a dozen "Foods That Can be Grown" that could serve as hog feed, including sweet potatoes, sorghum millet, corn, peanuts, "all sorts of garden vegetables," pumpkins, cow peas, and Bermuda grass.[3]

He concluded the bulletin with five "Things to Bear in Mind," including keeping the hogs' quarters clean and supplying the hogs with ample quantities of food and clean water. "For the curing of meat, making sausage, scrapel, souse and other choice dishes," he referred readers to his Bulletin No. 24, "The Pickling and Curing of Meat in Hot Weather" (1912).[4]

The next spring (April 1936), Carver published Bulletin No. 41, "Can Live Stock Be Raised Profitably in Alabama?"[5] The short answer to this question, of course, was that livestock could indeed be raised profitably in Alabama. In particular, he urged farmers to keep at least one cow, arguing, "For centuries a good, well-cared for cow was recognized as half of any family's living." Left unstated, again, was an answer to the question of how impoverished black southern tenant farmers and sharecroppers would find the money to purchase even that one cow. Once again, also, he called upon farmers to abandon the belief "that Alabama is adapted to cotton growing only" and, instead, to focus on growing corn, velvet and soy beans, peanuts, cow peas, alfalfa, sweet sorghum, and sweet potatoes.[6] That publication was followed in October 1936 with "How to Build Up and Maintain the Virgin Fertility of

Our Soils." This bulletin, too, was a re-articulation of earlier Carver arguments about producing maximum crop yields with the least outlay of money or injury to the soil.[7]

Meanwhile, there was a correlative effort emerging in the country that aimed to reverse the fortunes of afflicted Americans, Southerners among them. In 1935, in the depths of the Great Depression, a Harvard-trained chemist named William Jay "Billy" Hale coined the term "chemurgy." He meant by this term the use of farm products to produce plastics, paints, and other products, including fuel sources that could serve as alternatives to gasoline.[8]

The notion of using renewable farm resources such as corn, sweet potatoes, and other carbohydrates to produce fuel was an idea dear to George Washington Carver. During the late summer of 1935, a *Birmingham News* editorial, "The Use of Alcohol as Motor Fuel," attracted Carver's attention. In a letter to the editor, he praised the piece, proclaiming that it "struck one of the most outstanding dominant chords in the great commercial possibilities of the South."[9] Carver went on to write, "Alabama as well as many other sections of the South can furnish large quantities of suitable sacchariferous and starchy materials from which a high grade of ethyl alcohol can be made . . . we have sugar cane, sorghum, molasses, sugar beets . . . we have sweet potatoes, corn, wheat, rye, rice." He concluded by expressing the hope that "the production of ethyl alcohol from home-grown products and waste will be our next successful venture."[10]

Roughly one year later, a plant in Atchison, Kansas, began producing fuel alcohol derived from corn. Carver celebrated this development with another letter to the Birmingham newspaper, this time challenging Southerners "to catch the vision" and to "establish several plants throughout the South at strategic points wherever large quantities of starch and sugar producing crops can be raised." He added, "The slogan of every farmer . . . should be . . . 'Take care of the waste on the farm and turn it into useful chemicals.'"[11]

By the mid-1930s, of course, Carver had already spent decades trying to discover alternate uses for farm products. Christy Borth, the chronicler of the chemurgy movement during the 1930s, acknowledged Carver's work with peanuts, sweet potatoes, pecans, and other products. Indeed, Borth called Carver the "First and Greatest Chemurgist" in his 1939 book about the origins of the movement, and he devoted an entire chapter to Carver's work.[12]

The emergence of the chemurgy movement invigorated Carver and seemingly gave him a great deal of satisfaction, since it offered validation of much that he had been teaching and preaching about since his early years at Tuskegee. In June 1936, he penned a letter to T. Byron Cutchin of the Virginia-based *Peanut Journal* in which he asserted, "Now is the crucial time to chemicalize the farm." He continued: "We must not only make the farm support itself, but others as well, with a large manufactured surplus to sell to those who are not fortunate enough to own and properly care for a farm." Again, he called for the manufacture of many consumer items, including "[i]nsulating boards, paints, dyes, industrial alcohol, plastics of various kinds, rugs, mats and cloth from fiber plants, oils gums and waxes," and much more, all of which, he emphasized, "can be made from waste products of the farm." The challenge, he urged, should be taken up by "youth with creative minds."[13]

By 1937, Carver was receiving regular invitations to participate in chemurgic conferences. The first one he attended was in Jackson, Mississippi, in mid-April 1937. In writing to his longtime friend, Dr. M. L. Ross of Topeka, Kansas, Carver drew attention to the invitation to participate and reiterated what for him had become a familiar theme, an understated boasting that the invitation bespoke acceptance by whites: "Naturally, we as colored people feel very happy over it, as this is the first time that a colored person has gotten into a scientific body such as this."[14]

Carver addressed the conference on the afternoon of its first day with a talk he titled, "My Work." As was often the case, his presentation included a scriptural verse, in this case a quotation from First Corinthians: "Behold I will show you a mystery." He then proceeded to talk about the magic and mystery of the horse bean.[15]

It was at the 1937 chemurgic conference in Dearborn, Michigan, that Carver first met Henry Ford. Like Carver, Ford was a pioneer in the chemurgy movement. Early in his days as an automobile manufacturer, Ford began looking for ways to produce synthetic materials that could replace the heavy metal bodies of his Ford cars. He also sought fuel alternatives to gasoline that would power those cars. Long before either process was perfected, Ford famously predicted that someday most of the parts that went into the making of automobiles would be grown on farms.[16]

Unquestionably, Ford and Carver knew of and admired each other's work long before they met. As early as 1931, Carver wrote to Ford, praising his efforts to utilize farm products in the manufacture of automobiles and inviting him to visit Tuskegee: "If you should ever come near enough to Tuskegee Institute, I hope you will stop long enough to look through my laboratory and you will see some of the things you are predicting already materialized and others in a high state of perfection."[17]

The first meeting of Carver and Ford came at a luncheon in Detroit's Statler Hotel. Ford had invited a number of chemurgy pioneers, including Dr. William Jay Hale and Dr. Charles Holmes Herty, both of whom, like Ford, were white. Carver apparently took his lunch alone in the hallway, outside the room where the others dined. Various accounts of and explanations for this bizarre occurrence have been offered, ranging from a statement attributed to Carver that "some folks might object to my presence at the table" to a Carver associate's explanation that "that Carver's old hands were shaky and he didn't want to embarrass himself by dropping a precious teacup."[18]

Malcolm Bingay of the *Detroit Free Press* remembered some years later that he saw Carver in the hallway that day and asked him "why he was not at the speakers' table. 'It's nicer out here,' he smiled. 'Some people just do not understand, but I understand. They'll call me when they are ready for me.'"[19]

Bingay sat with Carver and talked with him about his vision of the chemurgy movement. According to Bingay, Carver told him, "God has ordained that there should never be any want, any poverty of any kind. All we have to do is follow His guidance and find his secrets. It's all so simple, if we could only understand."

Carver predicted to Bingay that "there will come a day when, out of the soil, we will make our houses, our clothes, our automobiles—everything on earth we need." Carver went on to say, according to Bingay, that "plant chemistry" was in its infancy and that "If wars are caused by the lack of things there will be no more wars because the earth will pour forth plenty for everybody. There will be no such a thing as a have-not nation." He added, "Mr. Ford understands that. That is why we began working together years ago."

On the surface, it might be difficult to understand Carver's adulation of Ford, especially if Ford was party to or even supportive of a slighting of Carver on account of his race. And yet, he clearly was smitten. Scarcely a month after the Dearborn conference, Carver wrote to H. A. Barnard, the Farm Chemurgic Council's technical director, to tell him, "I treated myself yesterday morning to a bit of unusual inspiration." The source of his inspiration? He drank his morning coffee from a cup that Henry Ford had given him! "Of course," he hastened to add, "I did not let anybody touch it for fear it would get broken. I took it back to my room immediately."[20]

Weeks later, Carver wrote to his friend M. L. Ross of Topeka, still ebullient over the time he spent with Ford: "The visit with Mr. Ford and being entertained by him was most notable. He is one of the most lovable characters that I have ever met, and we seem to have so much in common that we enjoyed each others company as but few men can."[21]

This characterization of Ford as a "lovable character" stands in stark contrast to the way much of the rest of the country saw him at this time. Carver's letter to Ford in the summer of 1937 came only weeks after Ford's henchmen had viciously beaten United Auto Workers organizers and their supporters at Ford's famous River Rouge facility in Detroit. Ford took a drubbing in the national press as a consequence, at precisely the time that Carver was finding him "lovable."[22]

On July 24, 1937, Carver wrote to tell Ford, "Two of the greatest things that have ever come into my life have come this year. The first was the meeting of you, and to see the great educational project that you are carrying on in a way I have never seen demonstrated before." The second of the "greatest things" was his opportunity to meet the British-born poet Edgar A. Guest, the so-called People's Poet, who immigrated to the United States in 1891 and worked for many years for the *Detroit Free Press*. Guest and Ford were friends, and Carver expressed the hope that both men might visit him together at Tuskegee.[23]

Ford sent Carver a note wishing him a Happy New Year in January 1938. Carver responded with a remarkably unrestrained expression of affection and admiration. He told Ford that his "personal greetings" were "far more precious to me than a very fine diamond I received." He went on to tell Ford, "believe me sincere when I say that I consider you the greatest man I have ever met." Carver offered three reasons why he felt this way about Ford, proclaiming him a man of great vision, a "great soul" who had "brought comfort and happiness to the whole world," and someone who was "in league with the Great Creator of all things."[24]

In part, Carver's highly affective letters may have been an attempt to fill the void in his life left by the departure from Tuskegee of Harry Abbott, a man who had served as his traveling secretary during much of the 1930s and also as his confidante and, arguably, his closest friend on campus. Carver quite simply loved Abbott, and he greatly appreciated the attentiveness and deference that Abbott showed him, gestures that both men felt were lacking in the way Tuskegee administrators and faculty treated Carver. In 1933, Carver wrote to tell Abbott, "I consider myself fortionate [sic] in being able to get you to accompany me on these many humanitarian trips we have made." He added, "You not only releived [sic] me of every responsibility connected with the trip but was [sic] always on the alert and seemed especially happy when you could add anything to my personal comfort which I appreciate far more than I have words to express."[25]

For all of his efforts to proclaim his attempt to be a humble servant of God, to serve the common good by allowing God to work through him, Carver's letters from this period evidence a troubled, somewhat unhappy man, who felt as though he lived among people who did not appreciate him adequately and did not do enough to pay tribute to him and his work. Abbott expressed this attitude clearly two decades after Carver's death, in 1964, when he donated a number of letters he had received from Carver to the George Washington Carver National Monument in Diamond, Missouri. In a cover letter to Monument officials, Abbott explained, "I do not intend to send any of the things I have to Tuskegee. I resent the way the younger (post-Moton) crowd treated Carver. He sensed it and that is one of the things he liked about me. I always felt very humble both with and away from him and I know how much he appreciated it."[26]

When Abbott left Tuskegee in 1937 to take a job in Chicago, Carver was crushed. The same month that he wrote to tell Ford that meeting the automobile manufacturer was the greatest thing that had ever happened to him, Carver wrote to tell Abbott that he had been ill and that he was "confident that some of my disabilities come from the fact that I can't see my friend Harry."[27]

Carver's letters to Abbott from 1937 on reveal a man whose health was declining, who was often depressed, and who was increasingly aware of his own mortality. At times, Carver seemed to solicit favors from Abbott, almost as if he was trying to test Abbott's continuing loyalty to him. At times, too, he was downright cranky with his old friend, especially when he thought that Abbott was not writing to him frequently enough or when he thought the letters were too short. In 1940, for example, after finally receiving a long-awaited letter from Abbott, Carver responded caustically: "Well you have relieved a most severe tension. I was almost frantic when I could not hear from you. I had all sorts of misgivings. In fact, I dreamed one night that your mother was dead and that was the reason you did not write. However, please don't let this happen any more."[28]

Carver continued to feel unappreciated at home, a feeling that made praise and recognition from the outside more welcome than ever, especially if that praise came from famous, rich white men such as Henry Ford. This, despite the fact that Tuskegee officials devoted the better part of an entire year, beginning in November 1936, to commemorating Carver's 40 years of service to the school. The festivities reached their climax on June 2, 1937, when a bronze bust of Carver, executed by the sculptor Steffen Thomas and paid for by donations from Carver's coworkers and friends, was unveiled on the Tuskegee campus. The speaker for the occasion was Dr. H. Barnard, director of the Farm Chemurgic Council, who declared, "Forty years ago [Carver] was actively developing the science of [chemurgy]."[29]

"The year 1937," Carver biographer Linda McMurry has written, "marked the beginning of what became a deluge of awards" for the aging scientist. Those honors included honorary membership in the National Technical Association and the Mark Twain Society, as well as feature articles on Carver in national magazines such as *Time* and *Life*. In 1938, a Hollywood production company brought out a film about Carver's life that included appearances by Carver himself.[30]

Despite the celebration of his career hosted by Tuskegee, Carver seemed to continue to harbor unhappiness toward the place he had called home for so long. In January 1938, he wrote Abbott, "I myself am getting much satisfaction out of the fact that people right here on the grounds let a stranger come in and see in a few bits of observation what they had not seen in years with reference to myself." He added: "The little narrow prejudices blinded their vision. It always does."[31]

Carver's spirits were lifted considerably in March 1938 when Henry Ford visited him at Tuskegee. He told his friend Harry, "the visit from Mr. Henry Ford cheered me up greatly." Carver told Abbott he wished the latter could have been there and proclaimed the visit, "a marvelous event in the history of Tuskegee Institute," adding cryptically, "[Mr. Ford] did not hesitate to say who He [sic] came to see, and he says he is coming back again next year."[32]

Over the next few years, Ford and Carver visited each other back and forth and remained in close contact. Two events especially pleased Carver. One was the dedication of a school named for Carver and built by Ford on his Ways, Georgia, plantation early in 1940. Again, Carver recounted the experience to Abbott in a letter and emphasized Ford's attentiveness to him: "I was with Mr. Ford the entire day. I don't think he left me fifteen minutes. . . . He rode beside me in the car, helped me over rough places, wouldn't let me walk anywhere, and kept people away from me."[33]

The other event, the one that sealed Carver's admiration for Ford for all time, came in the late summer of 1941. By that time, Carver's health had declined precipitously and he had moved from Rockefeller Hall to Dorothy Hall, the building that housed his laboratory and office. Aware of Carver's difficulty in walking up and down the steps that connected his lab to his living quarters, Ford purchased an elevator and oversaw its installation in Dorothy Hall. Carver was ecstatic. On September 29, 1941, he wrote to thank Ford in what stands as a classic Carver statement of hyperbole.

Addressed to "The greatest of all my inspiring friends, Mr. Henry Ford," Carver's letter proclaimed "the marvelous elevator you gave and had installed for me" to be "a *life saver*." He told Ford that in the few weeks he had been using the elevator, his health had improved

In a 1941 letter, Carver called automobile magnate Henry Ford the "greatest of all my inspiring friends." (Courtesy of the Tuskegee University Archives)

dramatically, a change he credited to Ford's gift: "The Great Creator will reward you. I cannot." Carver credited Ford with helping him "to do better work" and proclaimed, "The greatest gift I have ever received from mortal man is the time I met you the first time at Dearborn."[34]

Some two months after this letter, of course, the United States entered World War II, in the wake of the Japanese surprise attack on Pearl Harbor. It was a war, many believed, whose seeds had been sown in policies of economic nationalism and retribution that had emerged from the ashes of World War I barely two decades earlier. The new war, destined to last longer and be far more destructive than its predecessor, prompted Carver to call for a renewed effort of saving and self-sufficiency. In a letter to Ford, referred to now as "my greatest inspirer and Divinely ordained prophet," Carver implied that the world had gone awry and that something needed to happen to set it straight: "A crisis must come to shake the world, to wake it up. It is here now and the world is just beginning to realize it."

Carver expressed confidence that the Axis powers would be "smashed" and that a "rebuilding period must follow." "'Smashing the Axis' is to be expected," he wrote. "It is one half why you came into the world, and the other one half is to rebuild it and show people how to live." He made vague references to "your new fiber mixture" and also implied that he was assisting Ford with the production of synthetic rubber. He told Ford that his own contribution to the war and rebuilding efforts—"my little service," he called it—"will probably show its best in the soil and food work."[35]

Toward that end, he brought out a "Revised and Reprinted" bulletin that he called "Nature's Garden for Victory and Peace." In this publication, Carver argued that the war-induced vegetable shortage could be compensated for by turning to "Weeds [That] Are Good to Eat." The prologue to this publication contained a poem by Martha Martin titled "The Weed's Philosophy," as well as a quotation from the book of Genesis, 1:29: "And God said, Behold, I have given you every herb bearing seed, which is upon the face of all the earth, and every tree, in the which is the fruit of a tree yielding seed; to you it shall be for meat." Carver published this bulletin, he wrote, because he saw it as "an opportunity to render a service much need at the present time, and equally applicable to our coming rehabilitation program."[36]

That bulletin was followed by another, "The Peanut," published posthumously in February 1943, the month after Carver died, on January 5, 1943.[37] "The Peanut" was coproduced by Austin W. Curtis Jr., the man hired by Tuskegee Institute in 1935 to carry on Carver's work after Carver was gone. Although Carver had initially been leery of Curtis's hiring because he feared the young man might steal his secrets, and although he objected to the fact that Tuskegee paid Curtis more than it paid Carver, he eventually came to appreciate and even like Curtis, a Cornell University graduate, who dubbed himself "Baby Carver." In addition to partnering with Curtis to further his work, Carver also played an active role in establishing the George Washington Carver Museum to serve that same purpose on the Tuskegee campus. The museum was dedicated on March 11, 1941, in a ceremony that featured a keynote address by Carver's good friend Henry Ford. Carver left his entire estate, valued at more than $60,000, to the foundation that operated the museum, a final gesture of commitment to the cause to which he had devoted his life.[38]

By this time, of course, Carver's most creative work was behind him. For good or bad, he had allowed his celebrity status that began to emerge in earnest in the wake of his 1921 "peanut testimony" before Congress to distract him from his earlier work, and he spent a disproportionate amount of his time making speeches and public appearances, while also devoting attention to his "massage therapy" and the outpouring of correspondence that accompanied it. "The man farthest down" had taken a back seat to all of these activities. On the positive side, this publicity gave him and his work a visibility and popularity rivaled by few people of any race in America. He would be well remembered by many long after he was gone.

NOTES

1. George Washington Carver, "The Raising of Hogs: One of the Best Ways to Fill the Empty Dinner Pail," Tuskegee Experiment Station, Bulletin No. 40 (October 1935). All of the bulletins produced by George Washington Carver are available on Roll 46, frames 0002–0464, George Washington Carver Papers, microfilm edition, compiled and filmed by the National Historical Publication and Records Commission, 1975, Inman E. Page Library, Lincoln University, Jefferson City, MO. The original GWC papers and microfilm edition are housed at the Tuskegee Institute Archives in Alabama.

2. Ibid., 3.

3. Ibid., 4.

4. Ibid., 6–7.

5. George Washington Carver, "Can Live Stock Be Raised Profitably in Alabama?" Tuskegee Experiment Station, Bulletin No. 41 (April 1936).

6. Ibid., 3, 8.

7. George Washington Carver, "How to Build Up and Maintain the Virgin Fertility of Our Soils," Tuskegee Experiment Station, Bulletin No. 42 (October 1936).

8. Christy Borth, *Pioneers of Plenty: The Story of Chemurgy* (Indianapolis and New York: Bobbs-Merrill, 1939), 22–24.

9. "Dr. Carver Writes about a Southern Opportunity," *Birmingham News*, August 8, 1935, Roll 61, frame 0352, George Washington

Carver Papers, microfilm edition, compiled and filmed by the National Historical Publication and Records Commission, 1975, Inman E. Page Library, Lincoln University, Jefferson City, MO. Hereafter referred to as "GWC Papers."

10. Ibid.

11. George Washington Carver to editor, *Birmingham News*, October 6, 1936, GWC Papers, Roll 19, frame 0947.

12. Borth, *Pioneers of Plenty*, 226–40.

13. George Washington Carver to the *Peanut Journal*, June 11, 1936, GWC Papers, Roll 19, frame 0072.

14. George Washington Carver to M.L. Ross, March 20, 1937, GWC Papers, Roll 20, frame 1008.

15. The text of this speech by Carver on April 12, 1937, can be found on GWC Papers, Roll 46, Frames 0944–0953.

16. Borth, *Pioneers of Plenty*, 21–22.

17. George Washington Carver to Henry Ford, June 30, 1931, GWC Papers, Roll 12, frame 1190.

18. Quoted in Peter Duncan Burchard, *George Washington Carver: For His Time and Ours* (Washington, DC: National Park Service, 2005), 90–91.

19. Malcolm W. Bingay, *Detroit Free Press*, January 7, 1943, GWC Papers, Roll 51, frame 788.

20. George Washington Carver to H.A. Barnard, June 12, 1937, GWC Papers, Roll 21, frame 0137.

21. George Washington Carver to M.L. Ross, July 9, 1937, GWC Papers, Roll 11, frame 0610.

22. Steven Watts, *The People's Tycoon: Henry Ford and the American Century* (New York: Knopf), 453–54.

23. George Washington Carver to Henry Ford, July 24, 1937, GWC Papers, Roll 21, frame 0816.

24. George Washington Carver to Henry Ford, January 10, 1938, GWC Papers, Roll 23, frame 0406.

25. Quoted in Gary R. Kremer, *George Washington Carver: In His Own Words* (Columbia: University of Missouri Press, 1987), 79.

26. Quoted in ibid., p. 12.

27. Quoted in ibid., 80.

28. Quoted in ibid., 13.

29. Quoted in Linda O. McMurry, *George Washington Carver: Scientist and Symbol* (New York: Oxford University Press, 1981), 257.

30. Ibid., p. 258

31. Quoted in ibid., 81.

32. Quoted in ibid., 160.

33. Ibid.

34. Quoted in ibid., 161.

35. George Washington Carver to Henry Ford, December 18, 1942, GWC Papers, Roll 43, frames 1058–1059.

36. George Washington Carver, "Nature's Garden for Victory and Peace," rev. and repr., Tuskegee Experiment Station, Bulletin No. 43 (October 1942), 5.

37. George Washington Carver and Austin W. Curtis Jr., "The Peanut," Tuskegee Experiment Station, Bulletin No. 44 (February 1943).

38. McMurry, *George Washington Carver*, 296; Lawrence Elliott, *George Washington Carver: The Man Who Overcame* (Englewood Cliffs, NJ: Prentice-Hall, 1967), 243.

Chapter 13

GEORGE WASHINGTON CARVER IN AMERICAN MEMORY

> It is impossible for me to tell you how astonished I was . . . to get
> a copy of the . . . illuminating article on "The Sage of Tuskegee." As
> I read it . . . I became so interested that I forgot that it was about my-
> self.
>
> —*George Washington Carver, letter to Mrs. Ellen McBryde Brown*

George Washington Carver died after a lengthy battle with pernicious
anemia on Sunday, January 5, 1943, at Tuskegee Institute, the place
he had called home for nearly a half-century. A memorial service was
held for him five days later in the Tuskegee Institute chapel, followed
by burial near his old friend and nemesis, Booker T. Washington, in a
plot on the campus.

Testimonials honoring Carver's life, his work, and the meaning of
both poured forth from throughout the country. His old friend Henry
Ford told a writer from *Fortune* magazine, "I have never known a man
who knew so much about everything."[1] The *New York Times*, which
two decades earlier had carried an article criticizing Carver's scientific
method, reported on his death four times over a five-day period. On
January 6, 1943, the *Times* repeated what had, by this time, become

the common image of Carver: "Dr. Carver, paying no attention to his clothes and refusing to make money on his discoveries, simply devoted his life to scientific agricultural research, to enable his colored brethren to make a better living from the soil in the South." The *Times* quoted Carver as saying, "My discoveries come like a direct revelation from God," not commenting on the fact that it was this very sentiment that had resulted in criticism from the *Times* in 1924.[2]

Back in Missouri, the former slave state in which he spent the first decade and a half of his life, the General Assembly meeting in the State Capitol in Jefferson City unanimously passed a resolution honoring Carver. The resolution called attention to Carver's birth and early life in Missouri and to the fact that he was a "noted Negro scientist in the field of agricultural research and by his untiring and constant devotion to this work gave to the world great discoveries, among which were many uses for some of the lovely agricultural products and by the developing of such articles as ink, pigment, cosmetics, paper and paint from the valueless clay loam of the south." The resolution added the acknowledgment that "in all his long life of service Dr. Carver gave no thought to his own personal advancement of or [*sic*] personal gain, but worked only for the benefit and welfare of humanity."[3]

It was the perfect epitaph, one that George Washington Carver might well have written for himself. It was his life as he wished it to be remembered. Lost in the resolution's promotion and adoption was the irony that it was passed in the same statehouse that persisted in its support of the legal separation of the races when it came to public education. Racial integration in Missouri's public school system was still more than a decade away. The University of Missouri, the state's flagship institution of higher education, would not admit African Americans for another seven years after Carver's death, and then only after being forced to do so by the state's courts. In 1943, Missouri law still prohibited blacks and whites from marrying each other, and the state was still reeling from a heinous lynching that had occurred the previous year in the southeast Missouri town of Sikeston. The perpetrators of the lynching escaped punishment.

In Missouri's capital city, however, the "Negro scientist," a native son, was honored for his lifetime of achievement, even if he could not have found a place of public accommodation in which to stay, had he been alive to accept the legislators' praise in person. In that regard, George Washington Carver was a symbol not only of his own achievements but of the greatness of America. Where else in the world could a Negro, "the orphan child of a race that is considered inferior," a black Horatio Alger, rise from relative rags to riches, not just from slavery to freedom, but from obscurity to fame?

Governor Payne Ratner, the chief executive of Kansas, the state where Carver witnessed a lynching and was denied entrance into college because of his race, gave voice to the true meaning of Carver's legacy: he was, Ratner said, "an aspiring example of the best in American life." Carver's story showed America as it wanted to be, rather than as it was: "To every member of his race, Dr. Carver left a legacy of hope and a beacon light pointing to opportunities of the future." Carver's personal career, Governor Ratner proclaimed, demonstrated "that the Negro can climb to the heights." In short, institutional racism in America was not an obstacle to success. Rather, Carver's life proved that "this Negro scientist who was born of slave parents" had succeeded "by hard work and exalted vision" in rising "to the stature of one of the most outstanding agricultural research scientists in the world." Thus, Ratner asserted, Carver "represented the true spirit of this great country—where every citizen has freedom in all things, including freedom of opportunity." It was a perfectly stated rationale for America's leadership of the nations of the Free World against the Axis powers during World War II. And it was a sentiment with which Carver likely would have agreed. He had, after all, written to his friend William H. Holtzclaw only a few years earlier to tell him, "I am trying to get our people to see that their color does not hold them back as much as they think."[4]

Carver's life was likewise celebrated by President Franklin Delano Roosevelt, who telegraphed his praise and condolences to Tuskegee Institute president Frederick D. Patterson. "The world of science," President Roosevelt said, "has lost one of its most eminent figures and the race from which he sprang an outstanding member in the passing of Dr. Carver. . . . All mankind is the beneficiary of his discoveries in the field of agricultural chemistry."[5] Vice President Henry A. Wallace, who recalled his nearly lifelong friendship with Carver, also sent condolences. Predictably, the religiously oriented Wallace emphasized Carver's spirituality and religiosity: "When Dr. Carver died, the United

States lost one of her finest Christian gentleman. . . . Those who knew him best . . . realized that his outstanding characteristic was a strong feeling of the immanence of God. Everything he was and did found its origin in that strong and continuous feeling."[6]

It is important to remember that these "memories" of Carver did not just suddenly appear in the wake of Carver's death. Rather, they were shaped by decades of widely publicized accounts of his life and work, many, if not most, of which were encouraged by Carver himself.

One of his earliest would-be biographers was his old friend Helen Milholland from Winterset, Iowa, the grande dame of the choir who, along with her physician husband, John, had befriended Carver nearly a half-century before, during the early 1890s. Milholland began her work during the late teens or early 1920s, a book that was never completed. Although Carver's greatest fame lay ahead of him at that point in his life, he harbored no doubt about the worth of a book about him and his work. In December 1920, he wrote to encourage Milholland in her effort and to offer his assistance by "looking the manuscript over for you" if she wished. In a remarkable gesture of immodesty, he told her, "When I pass from earth to my reward there will be a great demand for such a book, and it will be a source of revenue for you in your declining years." He added, "To give it more value I might give to it my endorsement" and speculated that magazines might "pay for certain parts of it as an article that would be of interest to science or popular reading."[7]

Although Helen Milholland never finished her biography of Carver, he continued to encourage her to do so, telling her, as late as 1928, "By and by, before many years your manuscript will be most valuable as I will have passed on and then writers will be casting about to write more books, and make them complete."[8] Meanwhile, Carver's growing fame drew other writers who wished to write about him, especially in the wake of his 1921 testimony before the House Ways and Means Committee. In 1929, Raleigh Merritt, a former Tuskegee student who had become a Philadelphia businessman, penned a Carver biography that set the tone for writing about Carver for decades to come. This "authorized" biography, published by the Meador Press of Boston, Massachusetts, was titled *From Captivity to Fame, or the Life of George Washington Carver*. The book emphasized its subject's "early struggles and later triumphs" and called attention to all that Carver had accomplished "for the betterment of mankind."[9] The Carver who emerges from the pages of Merritt's book transformed southern agriculture and the lives of black agricultural workers, destroyed negative racial stereotypes, and demonstrated the power that individuals could exert if only they would allow God to work through them.

Although Merritt wrote in the preface to his book, "Dr. Carver prefers not to be made the subject of any biography," the opposite was true.[10] When Merritt seemingly tried to persuade Carver not to cooperate with other writers trying to write accounts of his life, presumably to give his own book primacy, Carver told him, "I would dislike very much to see you try to stop everybody else from writing." Indeed, he told Merritt, "You are not the first one by any means to attempt a book" and pointed out that he knew of seven ongoing attempts to chronicle his life.[11]

For years, Carver nurtured an image of himself as a wise, self-sacrificing servant of the common good, "the Sage of Tuskegee," as one publication dubbed him in 1936. Indeed, upon reading the article about himself by that title in the *Junior Red Cross Journal* in 1936, Carver wrote to the journal's editor, telling her, "As I read it a number of times I became so interested that I forgot that it was about myself." He added, "In fact, the story is so beautifully and interestingly written that it is hard for me to believe that it is about me. I lose that part of it."

In short, Carver was enthralled with his own life story, and he hoped and assumed that others would be as well. Revealingly, he told the editor, "One of our teachers was present when I opened it. He grew enthusiastic and set about at once to secure a copy for himself and his little reading room for the students under his charge."[12]

The work that solidified Carver's reputation and image as a man of God and as a spiritual seer was a small booklet titled *The Man Who Talks with the Flowers: The Life Story of Dr. George Washington Carver*, published in 1939. The author, Glenn Clark, was an evangelical Christian involved in the "Crusade for Christ" movement who met Carver through his "original boy," Jimmie Hardwick. In the book's foreword, Clark labeled Carver the "greatest Negro of modern times, if not of all times."[13] The gap filled by *The Man Who Talks with the Flowers*, according to its author, was that "it gives especial attention to interpreting the inner soul of the man and revealing the spiritual processes by which his remarkable discoveries were made possible. Among other things," Clark wrote, "it tells the secret of his power of talking to the flowers and letting the flowers talk to him."[14] The secret, of course, was that Carver had turned his life over entirely to God and had allowed God to speak to him through His creations.

The book that dominated Americans' thinking about Carver for much of the second half of the 20th century was a biography written by Rackham Holt and published by Doubleday Doran Press of New York only weeks after Carver's death, in 1943. Holt had begun work on the book during the late 1930s. She visited Carver multiple times at Tuskegee in search of material for the book, and she asked Carver to share written reminiscences of his life with her. The Carver who emerged from the pages of Holt's biography was a flawless hero of gigantic proportions. Holt's Carver suffered in silence, worked tirelessly, thought brilliantly, gave selflessly, and possessed such a sense of modesty that he spent much of his time in his later years fending off the compliments that his genius deserved.

Again, it was Carver's life as he wished it had been, not exactly as it always was, and he loved it. In 1940, Holt sent Carver a draft of the manuscript for his review. He was extremely pleased with Holt's treatment of his life, and he wrote to tell her so: "I want you to know that it is the most fascinating piece of writing that I have read. I started in and I confess I could not lay it down until I had finished it."[15]

Carver encouraged Holt at every opportunity and responded quickly to her requests for information, although he warned her that his early life memories were limited. He explained, "There are some things that an orphan child does not want to remember," a comment that seems at odds with other recollections of what he described as a generally happy childhood and a statement that no doubt served to accentuate the remarkable path his life had taken against all odds.

By the summer of 1942, Carver had become excited about the prospect of the publication of his biography. He wrote to tell Holt, "the calls that are coming in for it are simply remarkable. . . . I believe the book will receive a storm of applause." Two months later, after learning the book's publication date had been set for early 1943, Carver wrote to tell Holt, "I am very certain that the book will be one of the outstanding biographies that has come out recently. I believe that every soldier will want a copy."[16]

Soon, however, as his health began to decline more rapidly, Carver became concerned that the book was not being made available more quickly. He wanted the book to come out while he was still alive. On October 14, 1942, less than three months before his death, Carver wrote what turned out to be his last letter to Holt. In it, he stressed, "I wish so much that the book could be finished," adding cryptically, "I was hoping so much that this book could be finished before it had to close with something sordid," meaning, of course, his death.[17]

Unfortunately for Carver, Holt's book did not go to press until after his death, but its publication solidified his public image for generations to come. So, too, did the designation of his birthplace as a national monument.

Even before Carver's death, a movement to declare his birthplace a historic site emerged. In 1941, the St. Louis branch of the National Association for the Advancement of Colored People (NAACP) proposed a Carver birthplace memorial to Congressman John J. Cochran of Missouri. This effort failed because "such a monument to a living man conflicted with National Park service policy."[18]

The effort revived in the wake of Carver's death, with Melissa Fuell Cuther, an African American high school teacher and member of the Missouri State Association of Colored Women from nearby Joplin, Missouri, and Dr. Richard Pilant, a native of the southwest Missouri town of Granby, as its chief promoters. Pilant, a white Washington University (St. Louis) professor, and self-described promoter of interracial harmony, made his intentions clear in a letter to Secretary of the Interior Harold L. Ickes. In a very revealing statement, Pilant told Ickes, "this Memorial was pushed ahead in time of war, because its proponents considered it a war measure designed to furnish a worldwide symbol of racial goodwill . . . and a partial refutation of the most damaging accusations the Axis has been able to level against us in this war—charges relating to our treatment of the Negro."[19]

Within less than three weeks after Carver's death, a bill to make his birthplace a national monument was introduced into the U.S. Congress. After multiple amendments, a bill passed out of Congress

Soon after Carver's death, high school teacher Melissa F. Cuther (kneeling, center), with Professor Richard Pilant of Washington University (St. Louis), successfully launched a campaign to have Carver's birthplace designated a national monument. (National Park Service)

on July 14, 1943, with the support of such notables as Secretary of the Interior Harold Ickes, Senator Harry Truman, and Congressman Dewey Short of Missouri.[20] It was as if Americans could not wait to celebrate Carver and the meaning of his life.

Subsequently, the federal government engaged in a five-year effort to purchase the former Moses Carver farm site from an unwilling seller. Government efforts to condemn the property and take it through the power of eminent domain resulted in the cost of the land exceeding the amount authorized by Congress, a development that delayed the creation of the George Washington Carver National Monument and forestalled its opening until September 1952.[21] The formal dedication of the site occurred on July 14, 1953, with Secretary of the Interior Douglas McKay and Missouri governor Phil M. Donnelly among the crowd of as many as two thousand people in attendance.

Meanwhile, scholars largely ignored George Washington Carver. One of the most important books about the post-Reconstruction South ever written, C. Vann Woodward's magisterial *Origins of the New South, 1877–1913*, published in 1951, made no mention of Carver. Neither did Gavin Wright's *Old South, New South: Revolutions in the Southern Economy Since the Civil War* (1986) or Edward L. Ayers's *The Promise of the New South: Life After Reconstruction* (1992). Even Louis Harlan's two-volume biography of Booker T. Washington barely took notice of him. In *Booker T. Washington: The Making of a Black Leader, 1865–1901* (1972), Harlan referred to Carver as "an eccentric genius . . . noted for his quarrelsome nature, his loyalty to the school, and his deferential behavior to whites." Carver, Harlan contended, "lived a life of undeniable usefulness while out-Bookering Booker Washington."[22] Harlan gave Carver only slightly more press in the second volume, *Booker T. Washington: The Wizard of Tuskegee, 1901–1915* (1983), calling brief attention to his agricultural outreach work.[23]

The civil rights and black history movements that gained popularity and maturity during the 1960s and 1970s caused scholars such as Harlan to be critical of "accommodationist" African Americans like Washington and Carver. The ultimate expression of this sentiment can be found in the writing of a historian named Barry McIntosh, who published a seminal essay titled "George Washington Carver: The Making of a Myth," in the *Journal of Southern History* in 1976. Drawing upon previously unpublished sources, including a 1962 study that suggested that many of Carver's "discoveries" were overrated, McIntosh found little to remember or praise in Carver's career.

Five years later, a distinguished biographer and historian, Linda O. McMurry, wrote a more sympathetic and balanced book about Carver and his work, *George Washington Carver: Scientist and Symbol*. This book, published by Oxford University Press, praised Carver's accomplishments, pointed out his flaws, and focused attention on his role as an unwitting symbol of America's struggle with the issue of race.

The late 20th and early 21st centuries witnessed a rekindling of interest in George Washington Carver, particularly in his role as a nascent conservationist. Peter Burchard's book, *Carver, a Great Soul* (1998), drew renewed attention not only to Carver's mysticism and spirituality but also to his work as a visionary conservationist. Burchard elaborated on these themes in a work commissioned by the National Park Service, *George Washington Carver; For His Time and Ours: Special History Study—Natural History Related to George Washington Carver National Monument, Diamond, Missouri* (2005). And it is Carver the conservationist that is the subject of a 2006 doctoral dissertation by historian Mark Hersey, titled "'My Work Is That of Conservation': The Environmental Vision of George Washington Carver." No doubt interest in this aspect of Carver's life will be stimulated by a forthcoming book by Hersey, to be published by the University of Georgia Press.

A spate of Carver books for children and juveniles over the past two decades and more give evidence of the perception of Carver's enduring value as a role model for American youth. Indeed, a search of the Library of Congress's card catalog produces 62 titles of books on Carver in the category "juvenile literature." At least a dozen books about Carver for children were written during the 1990s, with another 18 titles produced between 2000 and 2010. The ecology theme is often repeated in these works, as is illustrated in a 1992 book titled *George Washington Carver: Nature's Trailblazer*, by Teresa Rogers. In a chapter titled "The Secret of True Happiness," Rogers wrote, "The message that George Washington Carver tried to convey, in the classroom and the countryside, was a message of ecology—the idea that everything in nature is part of one great whole. Whether he was talking about a vegetable garden or the human family Carver believed that we are part of a network of relationships."[24]

Arguably the most influential book for young students over the past three decades has been Eva Moore's 1971 book, *The Story of George Washington Carver*, published by Scholastic. Still in print after nearly three decades, Moore's book has no doubt influenced countless American school children in their understanding of Carver and his place in history. Perhaps the most important message of Moore's book appears in its last sentence, where she tells readers, "[Carver] had lived his life to help others, and that is the best a person can do."[25]

There is no denying George Washington Carver's desire to help others, especially the poor and downtrodden agricultural workers of the rural South. Nor is there any denying his conviction that God had empowered him with special gifts that allowed him to engage in this work. Less clear, and more controversial, is the actual impact his work and life had on black Southerners, then and now.

In popular culture, the image of George Washington Carver, the image that he nurtured, is that of a brilliant scientist who almost singlehandedly transformed the economy of the South while rescuing "the man farthest down" from a life of dependency and drudgery. In reality, neither of those things is true. In point of fact, neither the southern economy nor black southern life as a whole was dramatically changed by Carver or his work. As historian Mark Hersey has written, "Carver's campaign ultimately failed in its aim to lift African American farmers out of the desperate poverty in which they lived and restore the vitality of southern soils."[26]

Nor would it be accurate to say, as some of his biographers have, that Carver "destroyed negative racial stereotypes" and transformed race relations in the region and the country. The reality of the harsh struggle for civil rights in the South and the nation during the generation after Carver's death testifies to the resiliency and persistence of white racism.

This is not to suggest that Carver and his work did not affect and transform many, many individual lives. There is no denying the magnetism of his personality, the effectiveness of his teaching, or the persuasiveness of his rhetoric. In 1989, this writer tracked down and interviewed a number of Carver's "boys," his former students and former coworkers. More than four decades after Carver's death, these men and women were still awestruck by his accomplishments and by the impact he had on their individual lives. Quite simply, they loved him.[27]

Perhaps this is one of Carver's greatest legacies. His life stands as a testimony to an individual's power to influence for good the people with whom he or she comes in contact. Seemingly, no one who ever met George Washington Carver was able to forget him.

Carver left another legacy, as well, one that 21st century Americans would do well to remember. He taught, or at least tried to teach, all of us to regard the natural world around us as a precious gift that we have inherited, a gift that must be cared for and nurtured and passed on to the people who follow us in better condition than we found it. His admonition to avoid waste and find a second and third and fourth use for everything may have been his most useful and pertinent advice. He also taught us how to live frugally. He did, after all, spend the better part of five decades in a dormitory, rather than a spacious house. And he certainly did not spend an inordinate amount of money on clothes, as this description of him by a Washington, D.C., reporter in 1932 verifies: "As he straggled through the streets here yesterday he wore an ancient golfing cap, a saggy green alpaca coat and a pair of brown-checked patched trousers topping this color scheme off with a bright green necktie."[28]

We should not be too critical of George Washington Carver for his effort to shape his own memory or to seek recognition from humans for the work he was doing for God. His was a complex life with more than its share of confusions and challenges, insecurities and self-doubts. Perhaps the burden of being "an orphan child of a race that is considered inferior from every angle" remained with him all his life and took its toll. Likewise, the presence and persistence of hostility toward him at Tuskegee added to his insecurity. But so, too, did the capriciousness of white racism. Whites raised him and praised him, befriended and sustained him. But they also threatened him and oppressed him and subjugated and even killed his own people. Carver can be forgiven for latching onto a strategy to deal with the dangerous whimsicality of whites and their ways.

Sadly, the propensity to celebrate Carver's life has at times had more to do with the motives of those doing the celebrating than with Carver himself. For many Americans at many times, the celebration of Carver has also been a celebration of themselves. "Look at how great we are," they have seemed to say. "Only in America could a black man, a former slave, rise to the heights achieved by the likes of George Washington Carver."

No doubt, there is an element of truth to this claim. But the mythology surrounding Carver complicates our effort to understand and appreciate his true greatness. He should be remembered for what he did, for what he tried to do and why. As he told Booker T. Washington early in his career at Tuskegee in 1915, "No individual has any right to come into the world and go out of it without leaving behind him distinct and legitimate reasons for having passed through it." In touching so many lives in a positive way and in giving future generations a guide by which to govern their decision making, George Washington

Carver left behind "distinct and legitimate reasons" for having lived. That alone makes his life worthy of remembrance.

NOTES

1. Quoted in Steven Watts, *The People's Tycoon: Henry Ford and the American Century* (New York: Knopf, 2005), 485.

2. "Dr. Carver is Dead: Negro Scientist," *New York Times*, January 6, 1943, 25.

3. "Missouri Legislature Honors Memory of Dr. Carver," *The Call* (Kansas City, MO), January 15, 1943.

4. George Washington Carver to William H. Holtzclaw, October 27, 1937, Roll 22, frame 0389, George Washington Carver Papers, microfilm edition, compiled and filmed by the National Historical Publication and Records Commission, 1975, Inman E. Page library, Lincoln University, Jefferson City, MO. Hereafter referred to as "GWC Papers." The original GWC papers are housed at the Tuskegee Institute Archives in Alabama.

5. "Carver Rites Tomorrow: President Roosevelt Pays High Tribute to Negro Scientist,"*New York Times*, January 7, 1943, 19.

6. "Wallace in Tribute to Carver," *The Call*, January 15, 1943.

7. Quoted in Gary R. Kremer, *George Washington Carver: In His Own Words* (Columbia: University of Missouri Press, 1987), 25.

8. Quoted in ibid., 27–28.

9. Raleigh Merritt, *From Captivity to Fame, or the Life of George Washington Carver* (Boston: Meador, 1929), 11.

10. Ibid., 12.

11. George Washington Carver to Raleigh Merritt, March 25, 1930, Carver Papers, Roll 12, frame 0051.

12. George Washington Carver to Mrs. Ellen McBryde Brown, October 29, 1936, Carver Papers, Roll 19, frame 1139.

13. Glen Clark, *The Man Who Talks with the Flowers: The Life Story of Dr. George Washington Carver* (Austin, MN: Macalester Park, 1939; repr. ed., 2007), 3.

14. Ibid.

15. Quoted in Kremer, *George Washington Carver*, 30–31.

16. Ibid., 32.

17. Ibid., 32–33.

18. Anna Coxe Toogood, *Historic Resource Study and Administrative History: George Washington Carver National Monument, Diamond, Missouri* (Denver, CO: National Park Service, 1973), 57.

19. Richard Pilant to Harold Ickes, January 24, 1944, quoted in Toogood, *Historic Resource Study and Administrative History*, 56.

20. Toogood, *Historic Resource Study and Administrative History*, 57.

21. Ibid., 58–59.

22. Louis R. Harlan, *Booker T. Washington: The Making of a Black Leader, 1856–1901* (New York: Oxford University Press, 1972), 276–77.

23. Louis R. Harlan, *Booker T. Washington: The Wizard of Tuskegee, 1901–1915* (New York: Oxford University Press, 1983), 207–8.

24. Teresa Rogers, *George Washington Carver; Nature's Trailblazer* (New York: Holt, 1992), 65.

25. Eva Moore, *The Story of George Washington Carver* (New York: Scholastic, 1971), 96.

26. Mark Hersey, "'My Work Is That of Conservation': The Environmental Thought of George Washington Carver" (Athens: University of Georgia Press, forthcoming), 4.

27. Tapes of these interviews are housed at the George Washington Carver National Monument, Diamond, Missouri.

28. Undated and unidentified newspaper clipping, GWC Papers, Roll 61, frame 0153.

SELECTED BIBLIOGRAPHY

Blackmon, Douglas. *Slavery by Another Name: The Re-enslavement of Black Americans from the Civil War to World War II*. New York: Doubleday, 2008.

Borth, Christy. *Pioneers of Plenty*. Indianapolis: Bobbs-Merrill, 1939.

Brandenberg, Aliki. *A Weed Is a Flower: The Life of George Washington Carver*. Englewood Cliffs, NJ: Prentice-Hall, 1967.

Burchard, Peter Duncan. *Carver: A Great Soul*. Fairfax, CA: Serpent Wise, 1998.

Burchard, Peter Duncan. *George Washington Carver; For His Time and Ours: Special History Study—Natural History Related to George Washington Carver National Monument, Diamond, Missouri*. Washington, DC: National Park Service, 2005.

Carty, Ed. *George Washington Carver in Indianola: A Tour Guide*. Indianola, IA: Warren County Historical Society, 1990.

Carver, George Washington. *George Washington Carver Papers at Tuskegee Institute* (microfilm). Edited by John W. Kitchens and Lynne B. Kitchens. Produced with the assistance of and under the sponsorship of the National Historical Publications and Records Commission, General Services Administration. Tuskegee

Institute, AL: Division of Behavioral Science Research, Carver Research Foundation, 1975.

Clark, Glenn. *The Man Who Talks with the Flowers: The Life Story of Dr. George Washington Carver*. 1939. Reprint, Austin, MN: Macalester Park, 2007.

Dodge, Matt. "George Washington Carver: Kansas Homesteader." *True West* 31 (April 1984): 24–27.

Edwards, Ethel. *Carver of Tuskegee*. Cincinnati, OH: Psyche Press, 1971.

Elliott, Lawrence. *George Washington Carver: The Man Who Overcame*. Englewood Cliffs, NJ: Prentice-Hall, 1966.

Ethridge, Elizabeth W. *The Butterfly Caste: A Social History of Pellagra in the South*. Westport, CT: Greenwood, 1972.

Federer, William J. *George Washington Carver: His Life and Faith in His Own Words*. St. Louis, MO: Amerisearch, 2002.

Ferrell, John S. *Fruits of Creation: A Look at Global Sustainability as Seen through the Eyes of George Washington Carver*. Wynnewood, PA: Christian Society of the Green Cross, 1995.

Ferrell, John S. "George Washington Carver: A Blazer of Trails to a Sustainable Future." In *Land and Power: Sustainable Agriculture and African Americans*, edited by Jeffrey Jordan et al. Waldorf, MD: Sustainable Agriculture Research and Education (USDA), 2009.

Harlan, Louis, ed. *Booker T. Washington Papers*, vols. 1–14. Chicago: University of Illinois Press, 1972–89.

Hersey, Mark. *My Work Is That of Conservation: An Environmental Biography of George Washington Carver*. Athens: University of Georgia press, forthcoming.

Hines, Linda O. "George W. Carver and the Tuskegee Agricultural Experiment Station." *Agricultural History* 53 (January 1979): 71–83.

Hines, Linda O. "White Mythology and Black Duality: George W. Carver's Response to Racism and the Radical Left." *Journal of Negro History* 62 (April 1977): 134–46.

Holt, Rackham. *George Washington Carver: An American Biography*. Garden City, NY: Doubleday, 1943.

Hurt, R. Douglas, ed. *African American Life in the Rural South, 1900–1950*. Columbia: University of Missouri Press, 2003.

Jones, Allen W. "Improving Rural Life for Blacks: The Tuskegee Negro Farmers' Conference, 1892–1915." *Agricultural History* 65 (Spring 1991): 105–14.

Jones, Allen W. "Thomas M. Campbell: Black Agricultural Leader of the New South." *Agricultural History* 53 (October 1979): 42–59.

Jones, Allen W. "Macon County: From Reconstruction to World War I." *Tuskegee News*, March 15, 1984.

Jones, Allen W. "The Role of Tuskegee Institute in the Education of Black Farmers." *Journal of Negro History* 60 (April 1975): 152–67.

Kremer, Gary R., ed. *George Washington Carver: In His Own Words*. Columbia: University of Missouri Press, 1987.

MacKintosh, Barry. "George Washington Carver: The Making of a Myth." *Journal of Southern History* 42 (November 1976): 506–28.

Martin, Robert F. *Howard Kester and the Struggle for Social Justice in the South, 1904–77*. Minds of the New South series, edited by John Herbert Roper. Charlottesville: University Press of Virginia, 1991.

McMurry, Linda O. *George Washington Carver: Scientist and Symbol*. New York: Oxford University Press, 1981.

Merritt, Raleigh H. *From Captivity to Fame, or the Life of George Washington Carver*. 1929. Reprint, Boston: Meador, 1938.

Moore, Eva. *The Story of George Washington Carver*. New York: Scholastic, 1971.

Norrell, Robert J. *Up from History: The Life of Booker T. Washington*. Cambridge, MA: Harvard University Press, 2009.

Norrell, Robert J. *Reaping the Whirlwind: The Civil Rights Movement in Tuskegee*. New York: Knopf, 1985.

Perry, John. *Unshakable Faith: Booker T. Washington and George Washington Carver: A Biography*. Sisters, OR: Multnomah Press, 1999.

Ransom, Roger L., and Richard Sutch. *One Kind of Freedom: The Economic Consequences of Emancipation*, 2nd ed. New York: Cambridge University Press, 2001.

Rogers, Naomi. *Dirt and Disease: Polio before FDR*. Health and Medicine in American Society series, edited by Judith Walzer Leavitt and Morris Vogel. New Brunswick, NJ: Rutgers University Press, 1992.

Rogers, Teresa. *George Washington Carver: Nature's Trailblazer*. Earth Keepers' series. New York: Holt, 1992.

Toogood, Anna Coxe. *Historic Resource Study and Administrative History: George Washington Carver National Monument, Diamond, Missouri*. Denver, CO: National Park Service, 1973.

Watts, Steven. *The People's Tycoon: Henry Ford and the American Century*. New York: Knopf, 2005.

Wolters, Raymond. *The New Negro on Campus: Black College Rebellions of the 1920s*. Princeton, NJ: Princeton University Press, 1975.

INDEX

About the Author

GARY R. KREMER is the Executive Director of The State Historical Society of Missouri and the Western Historical Manuscript Collection. He is also an adjunct faculty member in the Department of History at the University of Missouri in Columbia. Kremer earned a doctorate in history from The American University in Washington, D.C. His previous books include an edited work, *George Washington Carver: In His Own Words*, and another biography, *James Milton Turner and the Promise of America: The Public Life of a Post–Civil War Black Leader*.